White Collar CRIMES X-Posed

Attention Authors

Manas Publications is fighting a war to tell the world that India can win the battle not only by the bullet but also by the pen. We are converting fighters into writers. There is no dearth of intellectuals in our country, however, their knowledge is confined to them only. No sincere effort has been made by any other publisher to give the right direction to their knowledge and the talent of every intellectual is lying hidden. An author always presents the raw material in the shape of a manuscript and it is the job of the publisher to convert it to a finished product. Manas has been continually motivating intellectuals and publishing their manuscripts for more than two decades and would like to publish your manuscript too. If you or your colleagues have a manuscript ready for publication or are working on it, contact us with a detailed synopsis and list of contents. Manas will also suggest you a suitable title for writing related to your area of expertise. Manas is known for its publishing quality. We take utmost care in publishing and also give wide publicity to the book and its author through our national and international distribution network.

White Collar CRIMES X-Posed

Thakur Shailendra Nath
Officer: Customs & Central Excise

Manas Publications
New Delhi-110002 (INDIA)

MANAS PUBLICATIONS
(Publishers, Distributors, Importers & Exporters)
4402/5-A, Main Ansari Road
(Opp. HDFC Bank)
Darya Ganj, New Delhi-110 002 (INDIA)
Off. © 23260783, 23265523, Res. © 23842660
Fax: 011-23272766
E-mail: manaspublications@vsnl.com
www.manaspublications.in

ISBN 978-81-7049-360-0
Rs. 595/-

Typeset at
Manas Publications

Printed in India at
Jaico Printers, Delhi
and Published by Mrs Suman Lata for
Manas Publications, 4402/5-A, Main Ansari Road
(Opp. HDFC Bank),
Darya Ganj, New Delhi-110 002 (INDIA)

CONTENTS

AUTHOR'S NOTE

It gives me immense pleasure to present my book titled 'White Collar Crimes X-posed' before the readers. The book brings together the famous criminal cases, IT and Bank Frauds... Money Laundering....issues relating to Direct and Indirect taxes and similar other interesting topics. The book provides some of the most important challenges faced by India. Crime and economy are co-related to some extent. In a crime free society economy grows by leaps and bounds. There is a commonality between current terrorism and global recession, both have spread their wings globally and are required to be tackled at a global level by taking co-ordinated efforts. At present, time and energy of the administration is greatly wasted in maintaining law and order. Need of the hour is to evolve such a system where there is equal participation of people and the administration in building a peaceful society. Inspiration, diligence, strong will-power and devotion are some of the properties through which sometimes a man performs unforgettable tasks. But the distressing conditions in three areas of our national life—internal security, public order and general law and order—show the machinery of governance in India, at the age of more than 60 years, that it is yet to learn the art of acting fairly, firmly and on time. Its soft attitude is reflected in what is known as the 'Broken Window Syndrome' in governance literature. If a window is broken and left unrepaired, people passing by will conclude that no one cares and no one is incharge. One unrepaired window automatically becomes an invitation to break more windows and lawlessness spreads outward from building to streets and then to the entire country. The tax evaders, criminals or terrorists, when caught, should immediately be given adequate punishment to show a lesson to others. There should be pure and pious judiciary who is able to exert itself while deciding a case and at the same time can pass an effective judgement. This would ensure the guilty realizing his mistake and will stop him from committing further crimes. It is the duty of the State to know under what circumstances and why one has committed a crime or an offence? Which were the social and economic reasons behind the criminal offence? And after completing his punishment is he suitably rehabilitated? Urgent police reform is very important. Presently ancient pre-independence system of police functioning is still prevalent, under which the only purpose of working was to please the British police officers. Now this old system requires a drastic change and the approach of the police work should be towards eradication of crime from the society. Recruitment procedure should also change, there should be only one entry point in police or other similar organisations and by virtue of their experience, intelligence and performance they should be promoted to a higher post. Extraordinary workers may be given outstanding promotions.

There is a global slowdown, reportedly the worst since the Great Depression of the year 1930. But India is least affected, in the sense, only from second half of the year 2008-2009, we have started feeling the punch of recession that too in real estate sector, and exports as it has declined since Sept 2008. After experiencing gross domestic product (GDP) growth at 9.4 per cent in 2006-2007 and registering an average growth rate of 8 per cent since 2004, India today faces a down turn, with the GDP pegged to expand between 7 per cent to 6 per cent in current fiscal. The real threat of slowdown in the short term is that which somewhat paradoxically presents an equally real opportunity for growth in the long term. As economies of the developed nations go into recession, the crisis presents an opportunity for emerging economies like India, to play 'catch-up', provided strategic planning is done. As rural areas are least affected by the current recession, the planning must prioritize rural areas for infrastructure and social development. It is primarily the infrastructure sector in India that may attract foreign investment. The required infrastructure developments are roads and highways, power plants and distribution, ports, airports, hospitals, education etc. Due to infrastructure development, there will be development in industries and manufacturing. The inflow of capital would create jobs and boost people's purchasing capacity. During the period of recession, there is a general tendency of savings for a secured future. To overcome this hindrance, coordinated efforts are required to be taken at global level by all the affected nations. Presently, they are giving stimulating packages at their own national level. The inflow of fund to the World Bank and Asian Development Bank is required to be substantially enhanced. Good governance is the lynchpin on which India's future rests, as much in short term as in the longer term.

I am really indebted and obliged to my department and my senior officers for their valuable guidance provided to me from time to time. I shall be failing in my duties if I do not express my gratitude to all the writers of books and articles published in various newspapers, which I have consulted while writing this book. I am very much thankful to Manas Publications, New Delhi, who have published this book. I give special thanks to Shri Manoj Gupta of M/s Gupta Computers of Gwalior for taking pains in typing this book.

I am also indebted to my wife and daughters, who have agreed to stay alone at Gwalior and allowed me to stay at NACEN, Faridabad and complete this book. One of my daughters, Anzuluica has even helped me in suggesting title of the book. I will appreciate criticism and suggestions from the worthy readers.

Thakur Shailendra Nath

INTRODUCTION

It is a fact that when you kill a man, you steal a life—you steal his wife's right to a husband and make her a widow, rob his children of a father. When you tell a lie, you steal someone's right to the truth. When you cheat, you steal the right to fairness.

An act is called crime because it is prohibited by the law. During the nineteenth century smoking was considered a fashion. Now smoking at public places is an offence. Use of opium by ladies at the time of child's birth was used to give relief to the mother from labour pain. In Chittorgarh area of Rajasthan use of opium is still prevalent and offered to guests as a sign of gesture, sometimes it is even considered as too sacred to be used as an evidence to keep promises but use of opium is prohibited under law and is considered as an offence.

White collar crime is generally committed by the white collar criminals having influence in society either through power or money. In white collar crime too much money is swindled. Their collar is white and always remains white even after committing the crime without getting any blot on it. White collar criminals are generally not engaged in criminal cases like murder etc but now-a-days the earlier position has changed and they are also engaged in murder etc through hiring someone. Literally white collar means "belonging or pertaining to the salaried or professional workers whose jobs generally do not involve manual labour." White collar crime is increasing day by day with the influence of computer and other advanced electronic technology and adoption of consumerism in the society. Businessmen are constantly discovering ways of influencing politicians and bureaucrats and engendering a whole new culture of disregard for the law of the land. They immediately obtain bail from the court or if they stay in jail, even procures five star facilities of comfort. Criminal minds have adopted noble modus operandi to become rich quickly. Recent example of Satyam scam is a manifestation of this trend. They spent money like anything causing immense loss to the economy. The middle class people of the society tries to copy them on the believe that even if Mr X has committed crime of murder, law could not do any harm to him.

The white collar criminals actively welcome the opportunity of corrupting others. With greed they look for politicians and bureaucrats who are amenable and there is no shortage of targets to stalk, so long as giving 'bribe' is not considered and seen as a crime in India, such white collar criminals will look for short cuts at every stage. They have indeed no choice, they will be left alone in the society, if they do not play an active part as a bribe-givers.

Definition

Crime is the breach of a rule or law for which some governing authority or force may ultimately prescribe a punishment. The word *crime* originates from the Latin *crimen* (genitive *criminis*), from the Latin root *cernō* and Greek κρινω = "I judge". Originally it meant "charge (in law), guilt, accusation".

A normative definition views crime as deviant behaviour that violates prevailing norms – cultural standards prescribing how humans ought to behave normally. This approach considers the complex realities surrounding the concept of crime and seeks to understand how changing social, political, psychological, and economic conditions may affect the current definitions of crime and the form of the legal, law enforcement, and penal responses made by society. These structural realities remain fluid and often contentious. For example, as cultures change and the political environment shifts, behaviour may be criminalised or decriminalised, which will directly affect the statistical crime rates, determine the allocation of resources for the enforcement of such laws, and influence the general public opinion. Similarly, changes in the way that crime data are collected and/or calculated may affect the public perceptions of the extent of any given "crime problem". All such adjustments to crime statistics, allied with the experience of people in their everyday lives, shape attitudes on the extent to which law should be used to enforce any particular social norm. There are many ways in which behaviour can be controlled without having to resort to the criminal justice system. Indeed, in those cases where there is no clear consensus on the given norm, the use of criminal law by the group in power to prohibit the behaviour of another group may be considered an improper limitation of the second group's freedom, and the ordinary members of society may lose some of their respect for the law in general whether the disputed law is actively enforced or not.

Legislatures pass laws (called *mala prohibita*) that define crimes which violate social norms. These laws vary from time to time and from place to place: note for example, variations in gambling laws. Other crimes, called *mala in se*, are nearly universally outlawed, such as murder, theft and rape.

Criminalization

- One can view criminalization as a procedure intended as a preemptive, harm-reduction device, using the threat of punishment as a deterrent to those proposing to engage in the behaviour causing harm. The State becomes involved because they usually believe costs of not criminalizing (i.e. allowing the harms to continue unabated) outweigh the costs of criminalizing it (i.e. restricting individual liberty in order to minimize harm to others).

- Criminalization may provide future harm-reduction even after a crime, assuming those incarcerated for committing crimes are more likely to cause harm in the future.
- Criminalization might be intended as a way to make potential criminals pay for their crimes. In this case, criminalization is a way to set the price that one must pay (to society) for certain actions that are considered detrimental to society as a whole. In this sense criminalization can be viewed as nothing more than State-sanctioned revenge.

States control the process of criminalization because:

- Even if victims recognize their own role as victims, they may not have the resources to investigate and seek legal redress for the injuries suffered: the enforcers formally appointed by the State have the expertise and the resources.
- The victims may only want compensation for the injuries suffered, while being indifferent to a possible desire for deterrence [see Polinsky & Shavell (1997) on the fundamental divergence between the private and the social motivation for using the legal system].
- Fear of retaliation may deter victims or witnesses of crimes from taking any action. Even in policed societies, fear may inhibit reporting or cooperation in a trial.
- Victims alone may lack the economies of scale which might allow them to administer a penal system, let alone collect any fines levied by a court [see Polinsky (1980) on the enforcement of fines]. Garoupa & Klerman (2002) warn that a rent-seeking government has as its primary motivation to maximize revenue and so, if offenders have sufficient wealth, a rent-seeking government will act more aggressively than a social-welfare-maximizing government in enforcing laws against minor crimes (usually with a

fixed penalty such as parking and routine traffic violations), but more laxly in enforcing laws against major crimes.

- As a result of the crime, victims may die or become incapacitated.

History

The earliest known civilizations had codes of law, containing both civil and penal rules mixed together, though not always in recorded form. The Sumerians produced the earliest surviving written codes, and it is known that Urukagina had an early code that does not survive. A later king, Ur-Nammu left the earliest code that has been discovered, creating a formal system of prescribed penalties for specific cases in 57 articles, the *Code of Ur-Nammu*. The Sumerians later issued other codes, including the "code of Lipit-Ishtar". This code contains some fifty articles, and has been reconstructed by comparison among several sources.

The Sumerian was deeply conscious of his personal rights and resented any encroachment on them, whether by his King, his superior, or his equal. No wonder that the Sumerians were the first to compile laws and law codes.

Successive legal codes in Babylon, including the code of Hammurabi, reflected Mesopotamian society's belief that law derived from the will of the gods (see Babylonian law). Many states at this time functioned as theocracies, with codes of conduct that were largely religious in origin or reference.

Sir Henry Maine (1861) studied the ancient codes available in his day, and failed to find any criminal law in the "modern" sense of the word. While modern systems distinguish between offences against the "State" or "Community", and offences against the "Individual", the so-called penal law of ancient communities was not the law of "Crimes" (*crimina*); it was the law of "Wrongs" (*delicta*). Thus, the Hellenic laws treated all forms of theft, assault, rape, and murder as private wrongs, and left action for enforcement up to the victims or their survivors. The earliest systems seem to have lacked formal courts.

It was the Romans who systemized law and exported it across their Empire. Again, the initial rules of Roman Law were that assaults were a matter of private compensation. The significant Roman Law concept was of *dominion*. The *pater familias* was in possession of all the family and its property (including slaves). Hence, interference with any property was enforced by the *pater*. The Commentaries of Gaius on the Twelve Tables treated *furtum* (modern theft) as a tort. Similarly, assault and violent robbery were allied with trespass as to the *pater's* property (so, for example, the rape of a slave would be the subject of compensation to the *pater* as having trespassed on his "property") and breach of such laws created a *vinculum juris* (an obligation of law) that could only be discharged by the payment of monetary compensation (modern damages). Similarly, in the consolidated Teutonic Laws of the Germanic tribes, there was a complex system of money compensations for what would now be considered the complete range of criminal offences against the person, from murder down.

Even though Rome abandoned its Britannic provinces sometime around 400 AD, the Germanic mercenaries – who had largely become instrumental in enforcing Roman rule – acquired ownership of the land, and continued to use a mixture of Roman and Teutonic Law, with much written down under the early Anglo-Saxon Kings. But only when a more centralized monarchy emerged following the Norman invasion, and the kings of England attempted to assert power over the land and its peoples, did the modern concept emerge, namely that a crime is not only an offence against the "individual", but is also a wrong against the "State". This is a common law idea, and the earliest conception of a criminal act involved events of such major significance that the "State" had to usurp the usual functions of the civil tribunals, and direct a special law or *privilegium* against the perpetrator. All the earliest criminal trials were wholly extraordinary and arbitrary without any settled law to apply, whereas the civil delictual law was highly developed and consistent in its operation (except where the King wanted to raise money by selling a new form of Writ). The development of the idea that it is the "State" dispensing justice in a court only emerges in parallel with or after the emergence of the concept of sovereignty.

In continental Europe, Roman Law persisted, but with a stronger influence from the Church. Coupled with the more diffuse political structure based on smaller State units, various legal traditions emerged, remaining more strongly rooted in Roman jurisprudence modified to meet the prevailing political climate. In Scandinavia, the effect of Roman law did not become apparent until the 17th century, and the courts grew out of the *things* — the assemblies of the people. The cases were decided by the people (usually largest freeholders dominating) which later gradually transformed into a system of a royal judge nominating a number of most esteemed men of the parish as his board, fulfilling the function of "the people" of yore.

From the Hellenic system onwards, the policy rationale for requiring the payment of monetary compensation for wrongs committed has involved the avoidance of feuding between clans and families. If families' feelings could be mollified by compensation, this would help to keep the peace. On the other hand, the threat of feudal warfare was played down also by the institution of oaths. Both in archaic Greece and in medieval Scandinavia, the accused was released if he could get a sufficient number of male relatives to swear him unguilty. This may be compared with the United Nations Security Council where the veto power of the permanent members ensures that the organization is not drawn into crises where it could not enforce its decisions. These means of restraining private feuds did not always work or prevented the fulfillment of justice but, in the earliest times, the "States" were not prepared to provide an independent police force. Thus, criminal law grew out of what is now tort and, in real terms, many acts and omissions that are classified as crimes overlap civil law concepts.

The development of sociological thought from the 19th century onwards prompted some fresh views on crime and criminality, and fostered the beginnings of criminology as a study of crime in society. Nietzsche noted a link between crime and creativity — in *The Birth of Tragedy* he asserted: "The best and brightest that man can acquire he must obtain by crime". In the 20th century Michel Foucault in *Discipline and Punish* made a study of criminalization as a coercive method of state control.

Natural-law Theory

Justifying the State's use of force to coerce compliance with its laws has proven a consistent theoretical problem. One of the earliest justifications involved the theory of natural law. This posits that the nature of the world or of human beings underlies the standards of morality or constructs them. Thomas Aquinas said: "the rule and measure of human acts is the reason, which is the first principle of human acts" (Aquinas, ST I-II, Q.90, A.I), i.e. since people are by nature rational beings, it is morally appropriate that they should behave in a way that conforms to their rational nature. Thus, to be valid, any law must conform to natural law and coercing people to conform to that law is morally acceptable William Blackstone (1979: 41) describes the thesis:

> "This law of nature, being co-eval with mankind and dictated by God himself, is of course superior in obligation to any other. It is binding over all the globe, in all countries, and at all times: no human laws are of any validity, if contrary to this; and such of them as are valid derive all their force, and all their authority, mediately or immediately, from this original."

But John Austin, an early positivist, applied utilitarianism in accepting the calculating nature of human beings and the existence of an objective morality, but denied that the legal validity of a norm depends on whether its content conforms to morality, i.e. a moral code can objectively determine what people ought to do, the law can embody whatever norms the legislature decrees to achieve social utility, but every individual remains free to choose what he or she will do. Similarly, Hart (1961) saw the law as an aspect of sovereignty with lawmakers able to adopt any law as a means to a moral end. Thus, the necessary and sufficient conditions for the truth of a proposition of law were simply that the law was internally logical and consistent, and that State power was being used with responsibility. Dworkin (2005) rejects Hart's theory and argues that fundamental among political rights is the right of each individual to the equal respect and concern of those who govern him. He offers a theory of compliance overlaid by a theory of deference (the citizen's duty to obey the law) and a theory of enforcement, which identifies the legitimate goals of enforcement and punishment. Legislation must conform to a theory of legitimacy, which describes the circumstances under which a particular person or group is entitled to make law, and a theory of legislative justice, which describes the law they are entitled or obliged to make.

Indeed, despite everything, the majority of natural-law theorists have accepted the idea of enforcing the prevailing morality as a primary function of the law. This view entails the problem that it makes any moral criticism of the law impossible in that, if conformity with natural law is a necessary condition for legal validity, all valid law must, by definition, be morally just. Thus, on this line of reasoning, the legal validity of a norm necessarily entails its moral justice. The solution to this problem is to admit some degree of moral relativism and to accept that norms may evolve over time and, therefore, the continued enforcement of old laws may be criticized in the light of the current norms. The law may be acceptable but the use of State power to coerce citizens to comply with that law is not morally justified. In more modern conceptions of the theory, crime is characterized as the violation of individual rights. Since so many rights are considered as natural, hence the term "right", rather than man-made, what constitutes a crime is also natural, in contrast to laws, which are man-made. Adam Smith illustrates this view, saying that a smuggler would be an excellent citizen, "*...had not the laws of his country made that a crime which nature never meant to be so.*"

Natural-law theory therefore distinguishes between "criminality" (which derives from human nature) and "illegality" (which originates with the interests of those in power). Lawyers sometimes express the two concepts with the phrases *malum in se* and *malum prohibitum* respectively. A crime *malum in se* is argued to be inherently criminal; whereas a crime *malum prohibitum* is argued to be criminal only because the law has decreed it so. This view leads to a seeming paradox, that an act that is no crime can be illegal, while a criminal act could be perfectly legal. Many Enlightened thinkers such as Adam Smith and the American Founding Fathers subscribed to this view to some extent, and it remains influential among so-called classical liberals and libertarians

Classification of the Crime

Governments criminalise antisocial behaviour — and treat it within a system of offences against society — in order to justify the imposition of punishment. A series of distinctions are made depending on the passive subject of the crime (the victim), or on the offended interest(s), in crimes against:

- personality of the State
- rights of the citizen
- public administration
- administration of justice
- religious sentiment and faith

- public order
- public economy, industry, and commerce
- public morality
- person and honour
- patrimony

One can also categorise crimes depending on the related punishment with sentencing tariffs prescribed in line with the perceived seriousness of the offence with fines and noncustodial sentences for the least serious, and (in some States) capital punishment for the most serious. Researchers and commentators may classify crime into categories like violent crime, property crime, and public order crime.

U.S. Classification

In the United States since 1930, the FBI has tabulated Uniform Crime Reports (UCR) annually from crime data submitted by law enforcement agencies across the United States. Officials compile this data at the city, county, and state levels into the Uniform Crime Reports (UCR) Violations of laws which derive from common law are classified as Part I (index) crimes in UCR data, and further categorised as violent and property crimes. Part I violent crimes include murder and criminal homicide (voluntary manslaughter), forcible rape, aggravated assault, and robbery, while Part I property crimes include burglary, arson, larceny/theft, and motor vehicle theft. All other crimes are classified as Part II crimes.

Analysts can also group crimes by severity, some common categorical terms including:

- felonies (US and previously UK)
- indictable offences (UK)
- misdemeanors (US and previously UK)
- summary offences (UK)

For convenience, such lists usually include infractions although, in the U.S., they may not be the subject of the criminal law, but rather of the civil law.

Crimes against international law

Crimes defined by treaty as crimes against international law include:

- crimes against peace
- waging a war of aggression
- crimes of apartheid
- piracy
- genocide
- war crimes
- the slave trade

From the point of view of State-centric law, extraordinary procedures (usually international courts) may prosecute such crimes. Note the role of the International Criminal Court at The Hague in the Netherlands.

Religion and Crime

Socially accepted or imposed religious morality has influenced secular jurisdictions on issues that may otherwise concern only an individual's conscience. Examples of activities that have been criminalized on religious grounds include alcohol consumption (prohibition) and abortion and stem cell research. In various historical and present-day societies institutionalized religions have established systems of earthly justice which punish crimes against the divine will and specific devotional, organizational and other rules under specific codes, such as Islamic Sharia or Roman Catholic canon law.

Military jurisdictions and states of emergency

In the military sphere, authorities can prosecute both regular crimes and specific acts (such as mutiny or desertion) under martial law codes that either supplant or extend civil codes in times of war.

Many constitutions contain provisions to curtail freedoms and criminalize otherwise tolerated behaviours under a state of emergency in the event of war, natural disaster or civil unrest. Such undesired activities may include assembly in the streets, violation of curfew, or possession of firearms.

Employee Crime

Two common types of employee crime exist: embezzlement and sabotage. The complexity and anonymity of computers may help sinister employees camouflage their crimes. The victims of the most costly scams include banks, brokerage houses, insurance companies, and other large financial institutions. Most people guilty of embezzlement do not have criminal histories. It is more likely that they have a gripe against their employer, have financial problems, or simply can't resist the temptation of a loop-hole they have found. Screening and background checks on perspective employees can help; however, many laws make some types of screening difficult or even illegal.

Some places of employment have developed measures in an attempt to combat and prevent employee crime. Places of employment sometimes implement security measures such as cameras, fingerprint records of employees, and background checks. Although privacy advocates have questioned such methods, they serve a good purpose to the companies using them. Not only do these methods help prevent employee crime, but they protect the company from punishment and/or lawsuits for negligent hiring.

Fear of Crime

The fear of crime refers to the fear of being a victim of crime as opposed to the actual probability of being a victim of crime. Studies of the fear of crime occur in criminology. The fear of crime, along with fear of the streets and the fear of youth, is said to have been in Western culture for "time immemorial". Fear of crime can be differentiated into public feelings, thoughts and behaviours about the personal risk of criminal victimization. These feelings, thoughts and behaviours have a number of damaging effects on individual and group life: they can erode public health and psychological well-being; they can alter routine activities and habits; they can contribute to some places turning into 'no-go' areas via a withdrawal from community; and they can drain community cohesion, trust and neighbourhood stability. Factors influencing the fear of crime include public perceptions of neighbourhood stability and breakdown, circulating representations of the risk of victimization (chiefly via interpersonal communication and the mass media), and broader factors where anxieties about crime express anxieties about the pace and direction of social change. There may also be some wider cultural influences: some have argued that modern times have left people especially sensitive to issues of safety and insecurity.

Affective aspects of fear of Crime

The core aspect of fear of crime is the range of emotions that is provoked in citizens by the possibility of victimisation. While people may feel angry and outraged about the extent and prospect of crime, surveys typically ask people how afraid they are and how worried they are. And lying behind the answers people give to these questions might be two dimensions of 'fear': (a) those everyday moments of worry that transpire when one feels personally threatened; and (b) some more diffuse or 'ambient' anxiety about risk. While standard measures of worry about crime regularly show between 30 per cent and 50 per cent of the population of England and Wales express some kind of worry about falling victim, probing reveals that few individuals actually worry for their own safety on an everyday basis. One thus can distinguish between fear (an emotion, a feeling of alarm or dread caused by an awareness or expectation of danger) and some more broader anxiety. However it should be noted that some people may be more willing to admit to their worries and vulnerabilities than others.

Cognitive aspects of fear of Crime

Concern about crime can be differentiated from perceptions of the risk of personal victimization (i.e. cognitive aspects of fear of crime). Concern about crime includes public assessments of the size of the crime problem. An example of a question that could be asked is whether crime has increased, decreased or stayed the same in a certain period (and/or in a certain area, for instance the respondents own neighbourhood). Between 1972 and 2001, the Gallup Poll show that American respondents think crime has decreased. By contrast, the cognitive side of fear of crime has increased and this includes public perceptions of the likelihood of falling victim, public senses of control over the possibility, and public estimations of the seriousness of the consequences of crime. People who feel especially vulnerable to victimization are likely to feel that they are likely to be targeted by criminals (i.e. victimization is likely), that they are unable to control the possibility (i.e. they have low self-efficacy), and that the consequences would be especially severe. Additionally, these three different components of risk perception may interact: the impact of perceived likelihood on subsequent emotional response (worry, fear, anxiety, etc.) is likely to be especially strong among those who feel that consequences are high and self-efficacy is low.

Behavioural aspects of fear of Crime

A third way to measure fear of crime is to ask people whether they ever avoid certain areas, protect certain objects or take preventive measures. This way, measuring fear of crime can become a relatively straightforward thing, because the questions asked tap into actual behaviour and 'objective' facts, such as the amount of money spent on a burglar-alarm or extra locks. However, it is important to note that some degree of 'fear' might be healthy for some people, creating a 'natural defence' against crime. In short, when the risk of crime is real, a specific level of 'fear' might actually be 'funcational': worry about crime might stimulate precaution which then makes people feel safer and lowers their risk of crime.

The influence of public perceptions of neighbourhood breakdown and stability

Perhaps the biggest influence on fear of crime is public concern about neighbourhood disorder, social cohesion and collective efficacy. The proposition here is that the incidence and risk of crime has become coupled in the public mind with issues of social stability, moral consensus, and the collective informal control processes which underpin neighbourhood order. Not only do these 'day-to-day' issues ('young people hanging around', 'poor community spirit', 'low levels of trust and cohesion') produce information about risk and generate a sense of unease, insecurity and distrust in the environment (incivilities signal a lack of conventional courtesies and low-level social order in public places); many people also use the language of 'fear' and 'crime' to express concerns about neighbourhood breakdown, the loss of moral authority, and the crumbling of civility and social capital.

People can come to different conclusions about the same social and physical environment: two individuals who live next door to each other and share the same neighbourhood can view local disorder quite differently. Why might people have different levels of tolerance or sensitivity to these potentially ambiguous cues? Research in UK has suggested that broader social anxieties about the pace and direction of social change may shift levels of tolerance to ambiguous stimuli in the environment. Individuals who hold more authoritarian views about law and order, and who are especially concerned about a long-term deterioration of community, may be more likely to perceive disorder in their environment (net of the actual conditions of that environment). They may also link these physical cues to problems of social cohesion and consensus, of declining quality of social bonds and informal social control.

Interpersonal communication and the Mass Media

Public perceptions of the risk of crime are no doubt also strongly shaped by mass media coverage. Individuals pick up from media and interpersonal communication circulating images of the criminal event — the perpetrators, victims, motive, and representations of consequential, uncontrollable, and sensational crimes. The notion of 'stimulus similarity' may be key: if the reader of a newspaper identifies with the described victim, or feels that their own neighbourhood bears resemblance to the one described, then the image of risk may be taken up, personalised and translated into personal safety concerns. In one study, subjects who received car crash information and who shared social identity with the victims provided elevated estimates of risk compared to those who had no basis for assumed similarity.

Yet the relationship between fear of crime and mass media is unclear, at least in its causal ordering. To put the dilemma in simple terms: do people fear crime because a lot of crime is being shown on television, or does television just provide footage about crimes because people fear crime and want to see what's going on? The complex nature of crime could allow the media to exploit social naivety, covering crime not only selective, but also distorting the everyday world of crime. Some say the media contributes to the climate of fear that is created, because the actual frequency of victimisation is a tiny fraction of potential crime.

With crime accounting for upto 25 per cent of news coverage, the quality and angle of the coverage becomes an issue. The media displays violent crime disproportionately, whilst neglecting minor crimes. The profile of offenders in the media is distorted, causing misunderstanding of criminal offending.

Unfortunately, however, despite an abundant literature on media effects – particularly the 'mean world' hypothesis – little work has been done into how representations, imagery and symbols of crime circulate in society, transmitted and transformed by multiple actors with a wide array of effects, only to translate into personal fears about crime. Perhaps future work will take account of the transmission mechanisms through which representations, beliefs and attitudes about societal risks are propagated in different social and cultural contexts.

Organized crime or criminal organizations

There are groups or operations run by criminals, most commonly for the purpose of generating a monetary profit. The *Organized Crime Control Act* (U.S., 1970) defines organized crime as "The unlawful activities of ... a highly organized, disciplined association...".

Some criminal organizations, such as terrorist organizations, are politically motivated. Gangs sometimes become "disciplined" enough to be considered "organized". An organized gang or criminal set can also be referred to as a mob. The act of engaging in criminal activity as a structured group is referred to in the United States as racketeering. In the U.S., organized crime is often prosecuted federally under the Racketeer Influenced and Corrupt Organizations Act (RICO).

Origins and conceptual background

"If we take a global rather than strictly domestic view, it becomes evident even crime of the organized kind has a long if not necessarily noble heritage. The word 'thug' dates to early 13th century India, when Thugs, or gangs of criminals, roamed from town to town, looting and pillaging. Smuggling and drug-trafficking rings are as old as the hills in Asia and Africa, and extant criminal organizations in Italy and Japan trace their histories back several centuries..." (Sullivan, Robert, ed. *Mobsters and Gangsters: Organized Crime in America, from Al Capone to Tony Soprano.* New York: Life Books, 2002).

"Piracy and banditry were to the pre-industrial world what organized crime is to modern society" (Paul Lunde, *Organized Crime*, 2004). Today, crime is thought of as an urban phenomenon, but for most of human history it was the rural world that was crime-ridden. Pirates, highwaymen and bandits attacked trade routes and roads, at times severely disrupting commerce, raising costs, insurance rates and prices to the consumer.

Organized crime is deeply linked to the moral problem of integrating subcivilized energy into civilized state building. The early Christian world was dubious about an unqualified legitimacy of nation-states. St. Augustine (City of God, 4.4) famously defined them as what would now be called kleptocracies, states founded on theft:

"If justice be disregarded, what are states but large bandit bands, and what are bandit bands but small states? ... Indeed, that was an apt and true reply which was given to Alexander the Great by a pirate who had been seized. For when that king had asked the man what he meant by keeping hostile possession of the sea, he answered with bold pride, 'What you mean by seizing the whole earth; but because I do it with a petty ship, I am called a robber, while you who does it with a great fleet are styled emperor' ".

A later North African writer, Ibn Khaldun, observing the predatorial conquests of the Mongol leader Tamerlane in the 14th century, developed a theory of state formation based on the periodic conquest of civilized states by barbarians, who are quickly acculturated by urban life, lose their warlike qualities and succumb in turn to conquest by yet another wave of barbarians (cf. Franz Oppenheimer's "conquest theory" of state-formation). As criminologist Paul Lunde states, "Barbarian conquerors, whether Vandals, Goths, Norsemen, Turks or Mongols are not normally thought of as organized crime groups, yet they share many features associated with successful criminal organizations. They were for the most part non-ideological, predominantly ethnically based, used violence and intimidation, and adhered to their own codes of law" (ibid.).

Although medieval feudal lords were not usually engaged in what moderns would consider "criminal activities" (except for irregular robber barons, self-enthroned Viking adventurers, and mercenary "free company" leaders), their hierarchical courts, monopoly of violence, extension of protection to their serfs in exchange for labour and a percentage of harvests and durability are structurally similar to classic organized crime groups like the Mafia. In the modern world, it is difficult to distinguish some corrupt and lawless governments from organized crime gangs. These regimes, characteristic of some of the newly independent states of the former Soviet Union, use the state apparatus to control organized crime for their own ends.

Organized crime dynamics

In order for a criminal organization to prosper, some degree of support is required from the society in which it lives. Thus, it is often necessary to corrupt some of its respected members, most commonly achieved through bribery, blackmail, and the establishment of symbiotic relationships with legitimate businesses. Judicial and police officers and legislators are especially targeted for control by organized crime via bribes. The famous dacoit Man Singh of Chambal (Gwalior, M.P.) used to help the poors from his loot in their daughter's marriage. He was a man of character and was very popular among the poor of the surrounding area. Similarly the famous Sandal Wood Smuggler Veerappan used to help the villagers in case of need who always helped him in hiding from police. The obliged villagers never used to give the whereabouts of their godfather Veerappan.

Lacking much of the paperwork that is common to legitimate organizations, criminal organizations can usually evolve and reorganize much more quickly when the need arises. They are quick to capitalize on newly-opened markets, and quick to rebuild themselves under another guise when caught by authorities. This is especially true of organized groups that engage in human trafficking.

The newest growth sectors for organized crime are identity theft and online extortion. These activities are troubling because they discourage consumers from using the Internet for e-commerce. E-commerce was supposed to level the playing ground between small and large businesses, but the growth of online organized crime is leading to the opposite effect; large businesses are able to afford more bandwidth (to resist denial-of-service attacks) and superior. Furthermore, organized crime using the Internet is much harder to trace down for the police (even though they increasingly deploy cybercops) since police forces and law enforcement agencies in general operate on a national level while the Internet makes it easy and simple for criminal organizations to cross boundaries and even to operate completely remotely.

In the past criminal organizations have naturally limited themselves by their need to expand. This has put them in competition with each other. This competition, often leading to violence, uses valuable resources such as manpower (either killed or sent to prison), equipment and finances. In the United States, the Irish Mob boss of the Winter Hill Gang (in the 1980s) turned informant for the Federal Bureau of Investigation (FBI). He used this position to eliminate competition and consolidate power within the city of Boston which led to the imprisonment of several senior organized crime figures including Gennaro "Jerry" Anguilo underboss of the Patriarca crime family. Infighting sometimes occurs within an organization, such as the Castellamarese war of 1930-31 and the Boston Irish Mob Wars of the 1960s and 1970s.

Today criminal organizations are increasingly working together, realizing that it is better to work in cooperation rather than in competition with each other. This has led to the rise of global criminal organizations such as Mara Salvatrucha. The Sicilian Mafia in the U.S. have had links with organized crime groups in Italy such as the Camorra the 'Ndrangheta and the Sacra Corona Unita. The Sicilian Mafia has also been known to work with the Irish Mob (John Gotti of the Gambino family and James Coonan of the Westies are known to have worked together, with the Westies operating as a contract hit squad for the Gambino family after they helped Coonan come to power), the Japanese Yakuza and the Russian Mafia. The FBI estimates that global organized crime makes $1 trillion per year.

This rise in cooperation between criminal organizations has meant that law enforcement agencies are increasingly having to work together. The FBI operates an organized crime section from its headquarters in Washington and is known to work with other national (e.g. Polizia di Stato and the Royal Canadian Mounted Police), federal (e.g., Drug Enforcement Administration and the United States Coast Guard), state (e.g., Massachusetts State Police Special Investigation Unit and the New York State Police Bureau of Criminal Investigation) and city (e.g., New York Police Department Organized Crime Unit and the Los Angeles Police Department Special Operations Division) law enforcement agencies.

Notable criminal organizations

Perhaps the best known criminal organizations are the Sicilian and American Cosa Nostra, most commonly known as the Mafia. The Neopolitan Camorra, the Calabrian Ndrangheta, and the Apulian Sacra Corona Unita are similar Italian organized crime groups. Other organized crime groups include the Russian mafia, Mexican and Colombian Drug Cartels, the Indian Mafia, Irish Mob, the Japanese Yakuza, the Chinese Triads and other crime syndicates. On a lower level in the criminal food chain are many street gangs, such as the Surenos, Nortenos, Latin Kings, Bloods, and Crips.

Recent notable criminal organisations are:

Al-Qaeda – Trades in opium and heroin, mainly engaged in Afghanistan.

LTTE — In Sri Lanka deals in heroin and cannabis, and trying to establish separate Tamil state in Sri Lanka. Recently Sri Lankan Army has killed its leader Prabhakaran and uprooted the gang.

PKK— Turkey indulges in Golden Crescent to Europe.

Palestine — Procures its finance through trade in Hasish and Heroin.

FARC — In Columbia deals with cocain.

NAXAL — In India is the extension of the Left Wing (Communist Party), has spread its Wing in Andhra, Bihar, Chhattisgarh.

Criminal organizations may function both inside and outside of prison, such as the Mexican Mafia, Folk Nation, and the Brazilian PCC. Biker gangs such as the Hells Angels may also be involved in organized crime.

Terrorist and paramilitary organizations such as the Provisional Irish Republican Army, Ulster Defence Association, FARC and the PKK have been known to engage in organized crime to raise funds for their political activities.

World leaders throughout history who have been accused of running their country like a criminal organization include Adolf Hitler of Germany, Idi Amin of Uganda, Mobutu Sese Seko of Zaire, Nicolae Ceaúlescu of Romania, Francisco Franco of Spain, Hugo Banzer of Bolivia, Kim Jong Il of North Korea, Slobodan Milosevic of Serbia and Yugoslavia, Alberto Fujimori of Peru (in league with his advisor Vladimiro Montesinos), Than Shwe of Burma (also known as Myanmar) and various other dictators and military juntas. Corrupt political leaders may have links to existing organized crime groups, either domestic or international, or else may simply exercise power in a manner that duplicates the functioning and purpose of organized crime.

Human rights law

Another use of the term "criminal organization" exists in human rights law and refers to an organization which has been found guilty of crimes against humanity. Once an organization has been determined to be a criminal organization, one must only demonstrate that an individual belonged to that organization to be punished and not that the individual actually individually committed illegal acts.

This concept of the criminal organization came into being during the Nuremberg Trials. Several public sector organizations of Nazi Germany such as the SS and Gestapo were judged to be criminal organizations, while other organizations such as the German Army High Command were indicted but acquitted of charges.

This conception of criminal organizations was, and continues to be, controversial, and has not been used in human rights law since the trials at Nuremberg.

Ideological crime

In addition to what is considered traditional organized crime involving direct crimes of fraud swindles, scams, racketeering and other RICO predicate acts motivated for the accumulation of monetary gain, there is also non-traditional organized crime which is engaged in for political or ideological gain or acceptance. Such crime groups are often labeled terrorist organizations and include groups such as Al-Qaeda, Hamas, Kach and Kahane Chai and the Jewish Defense League

Typical activities

Organized crime often victimize businesses through the use of extortion or theft and fraud activities like hijacking cargo trucks, robbing goods, committing bankruptey fraud (also known as "bust-out"), insurance fraud or stock fraud (inside trading). Organized crime groups also victimize individuals by car theft (either for dismantling at "Chop shops" or for export), burglary, credit card fraud, and stock fraud ("pump and dump" scam). Some organized crime groups defraud national, state, or local governments by bid-rigging public projects, counterfeiting money, smuggling or manufacturing untaxed alcohol (bootlegging) or cigarettes (buttlegging), and providing immigrant workers to avoid taxes. Organized crime groups seek out corrupt public officials in executive, law enforcement, and judicial departments so that their activities can avoid, or at least receive early warnings about, investigation and prosecution.

Organized crime groups also provide a range of illegal services and goods, such as loansharking of money at very high interest rates, bookmaking and gambling, prostitution, drug trafficking, gunrunning, providing murder for hire, illegal dumping of toxic waste, people smuggling and trafficking in human beings. Organized crime groups also do a range of business and labour racketeering activities, such as casino skimming, insider trading, setting up monopolies in industries such as garbage collecting, construction and cement pouring, bid rigging, getting "no-show" and "no-work" jobs, using non-union labour and pocketing the wage difference, money laundering, political corruption, bullying and ideological clamping.

Is it feasible to make CBI an FBI?

The recommendation of the Parliamentary panel to bestow on the CBI the same status as the FBI of the US has focused attention on an important issue. In 1997 in the hawala case, after noticing the report of the Independent Review Committee of the Central Government, the apex court had strongly advocated insulation of the CBI from executive, political and extraneous influence.

Now, the Parliamentary panel's recommendation is a belated step to free the CBI from executive or political interference and is also recognition of the enormity of the challenges of terrorism and hi-tech crimes that face the nation. Presently, the CBI works as per the Delhi Special Police Establishment Act, 1946, which means the Central Government exercises superintendence over it. Functioning of the CBI in the states is contingent upon the respective states granting consent to it.

In its present shape CBI lacks independence, infrastructure and the legal competence to engage in tasks like FBI, which was established in 1908 as the Bureau of Investigation. Under a 1968 legislation its directors are appointed by the US President subject to confirmations by the US Senate and the maximum tenure is fixed as ten years. What has to be considered is the desirability of investing the CBI with the kind of authority the FBI has, in view of our federal structure.

CHAPTER 1 BANKING FRAUDS

BANK SECRET DEAL WITH COMPANY

As the derivatives battle rages on, there will be a chink in bank's armour or so their warring corporate clients think. This is the distinguished premium that derivative banks have paid to corporates to help them make a fast buck. Deals were structured in a way to mask such receipt of premium by corporate – a transaction that RBI rules ban. Shaken by derivatives blows, many corporates are wielding this as a weapon in their last ditch attempts at legal recourse.

Once a corporate moves court, it is spared of making provision for the derivative loses in its books, a measure that would help it overcome the recent accounting directions impact. Many corporates have already moved courts and other are exploring legal options.

In the world of synthetic over the counter derivatives, premium is earned by the option writer (i.e. the option sector). Writing options, where the return is only a fixed premium but the possible loss is unlimited, being a risky business, corporate are barred and only bank can write options. So a corporate cannot directly get a premium cheque from the bank. To side step this, the bank through a strict heart deal to the corporate. This could be in the form of an attractive, off market exchange rate – like, agreeing to buy dollars from the exporter at higher rate when the spot market rate is lower. Banks devise zero cost structures under which a corporate seeks an option and buys another so the net premium received by the corporate is nil. But while it is an open secret in the banking circle that such deals are simply cut to duck the restriction, there are doubts whether it can be substantiated in court. The transaction look like any normal currency hedge, even to argue that there is an intent of hiding the option premium one has to track the rates and raise the question as to whether it was rational for the banks to do so.

RELAXATIONS OF CURBS ON FOREIGN FLOWS

Review of restrictions imposed on small and medium size firm seeking to borrow from abroad for expenditure of rupee is required as these restrictions were imposed when the economy was faced with dollar deluge. Excess domestic money supply – M3 growth – caused by deluge of dollars has gone a way beyond the target set by the RBI. Aggregate capital inflows into the economy through various channels such as portfolio, external commercial borrowing (ECB), FDI etc. have crossed $100 billion. So fearing excess liquidity in the system, the government and the central bank chose to clamp down on foreign borrowing by SME for rupee expenditure. At present a company cannot raise more than $20 million abroad for rupee expenditure. Borrowing below that threshold can also be done only after prior approval by the RBI, while such curbs on borrowings may have had some rationale in 2007, the situation seem to have changed in 2008. Capital flows are not robust as they were in 2007. The rupee is also not under so much pressure to appreciate. Lenders abroad, specially in the US and the EU are far more circumspect after the mortgage and subprime crises and resultant credit crunch in the US.

Given these changed circumstances it might make sense for the government to relax the ECB norms. The only reason why the government may still be reluctant to open up its window is the continuing inflationary pressure. But the RBI needs to strike a balance between the macro imperative of keeping sources of additional liquidity in check and the genuine need of the SME to borrow from abroad. The RBI will also have to ensure that small companies have enough credit supply at cheaper rates, especially in the backdrop of fears of a slowdown in the economy. Smaller companies form the backbone of economy and it makes sense to allow them to borrow cheaper in small quantity from abroad to meet rupee expenditure. This will also help correct the domestic bank lending system which may be somewhat skewed against the small borrower at present.

Financial intelligence

Fundamentally financial intelligence boils down to four distinct skill sets. One, understanding the foundation. Managers who are financially intelligent understand the basis of financial measurement. They can read an income statement, a balance sheet, and a cash flow statement. They know the difference between profit and cash. They understand why balance sheet balances. The numbers neither scare nor mystify them.

Financially intelligent managers are able to identify where the artful aspects of finance have been applied to the numbers, and they know how applying them differently might lead to different conclusion. Financially intelligent managers don't shrink from ratio, return on investment analysis and the like. Factors such as the economy, the competitive environment, regulations, changing customers needs and expectation and new technology all affect how numbers are interpreted and what decision should be made.

Curb ECS misuse

The RBI needs to curb misuse of electronic clearing service (ECS) debit facility. Many leading private and foreign banks are taking undue advantage of ECS debit facility, and sufferers are public sector banks (PSB). If balance in an account is not sufficient to ECS debit, then the same has to be intimated to the clearing centre immediately. When ECS debits come in the morning, at the same time clearing charges statements are also received for debiting customers account by the bank branch. In the meantime branches fail to intimate ECS debit returns and these private foreign banks refuse to accept late ECS debit returns. Thus PSB are forced to debit the accounts resulting in debit balance. The RBI should either extend time to intimate dishonoured ECS debits or stop ECS debit clearing.

(a) INTERNET BANKING FRAUD

Internet Banking Fraud is a fraud or theft committed by using online technology to illegally remove money from a bank account and/or transfer money to an account in a different bank. Internet Banking Fraud is a form of identity theft and is usually made possible through techniques such as phishing.

Once the police in India announced that they had recovered 1 million Indian Rupees (almost US$23,000) in funds allegedly stolen from Citibank customers in the U.S. by employees of an Indian call center firm.

The case highlights the need for a reexamination of corporate cultures and corporate ethics, as well as the sorry state of the Indian judicial system that serves as an impediment to international business and to individual safety and security there. It also emphasizes that U.S. enforcement agencies must adapt to new high-tech fraud activities conducted from offshore locations.

The experience of Citibank could prompt some U.S. clients to consider changes in their outsourcing operations in India.

The announcement about the recovery of funds came a day after it was announced that three former employees of Indian call center firm MphasiS BFL and nine alleged accomplices were being held on suspicion of stealing $350,000 (over 15 million Rupees) from four Citibank customers in the U.S.

Police in Pune, Maharashtra, said that 1 million Rupees were recovered from the home of a relative of Ivin Samuel Thomas, 30, a former employee of Msource, a call center in Pune that is a subsidiary of MphasiS BFL.

How the Fraud is Operated

One former employee is being portrayed in local press reports in India as the ringleader who organized the fraud operation against MphasiS' Citibank customers. Two other MphasiS employees reportedly arrested are Siddhartha Subhash Mehta, 20, and Stephen Daniel, 24. The other nine individuals arrested were reportedly not MphasiS employees.

Police officials in Pune said that the three MphasiS employees were customer service agents who came into contact with U.S. customers who called into the MphasiS call center for help with their Citibank accounts.

The trio gained the confidence of four U.S. customers and obtained PIN numbers and other account information, which was then used to transfer money out of those customers' accounts into the accounts of members of the gang. Police reports said that the three worked as account representatives at MphasiS for six months, ending in December 2004.

Auditing Fraud — A SAI India Experience

In recent times the Comptroller and Auditor General of India audited a series of fraudulent drawls of public funds in a provincial government. These drawls amounting to Rs. 6500 million occurred during 1990-96 and related to the Animal Husbandry department of that government.

Audit investigations were prompted by the following:

- Annual financial statements and appropriation accounts of several years showed that the Animal Husbandry department had made large scale excess drawls over and above their authorised budgets.
- Unexplained and unjustified increase in purchases of cattle feed, fodder, medicines and veterinary equipment were noticed.

- Preliminary examination of records provided evidence of subversion of internal control mechanisms.
- Media reports.
- Public interest litigations had been filed before the High Court of the province.
- Police action had been initiated in some cases in early 1996.
- The provincial government had shown vulnerability to fraud as it had been reluctant to ensure timely submission of initial accounts and had been lukewarm in its response to earlier reports of the CAG of India.

Though the fraud essentially involved drawl of money against bills based on fake invoices by officials of the Animal Husbandry Department, connivance of officials of the Treasury and Finance departments were probable.

Audit Strategy

In view of the strong evidence of extensive subversion of internal controls and established procedures, reliance was placed on direct substantive testing. Nearly 9000 vouchers and 0.35 million sub-vouchers were compiled into a database. It was also decided to extensively document and report on the breakdown of internal controls and subversion of procedures relating to purchases, budgetary and expenditure control, and the drawl and disbursement of funds. The role of officials in departments, such as Finance, District Administration, Treasury, Vigilance and Sales Tax, who could have connived in the systematic fraudulent drawl of funds was also to be examined.

Constraints

- Large non-computerised volumes of data were to be audited.
- Audit staff had limited previous experience of investigating fraudulent transactions.

- Audit offices were dispersed and located at considerable distances away from the audit office.
- Since the fraud was also being investigated by a Federal Investigating agency key officials were not easily available for discussion as many were in custody. Further, a number of vital records had also been seized by the investigating agency and were therefore not easily available for audit examination.
- A large number of audit teams were deployed and this raised coordination issues.
- The possible connivance of the top political leadership in the fraud led to reluctance on the part of key officials in coming forward with information.
- Threats existed to the personal safety of audit officials.
- The ongoing criminal investigations placed a heavy demand on senior audit officials for information thereby affecting the pace of audit work.
- There was pressure from the media to provide information on audit findings.

Audit Approach

In view of the constraints detailed above, several innovations had to be built into the audit approach. The more significant of these are:

- A database was created of purchase and payroll vouchers and sub-vouchers. This facilitated analysis and review of the fraudulent payments and provided insights into new aspects of the fraud.
- The skills of the auditors were supplemented through close supervision and monitoring to cover the lack of adequate guidelines for auditing fraud.
- To keep audit findings confidential the standard practice of issuing preliminary observations was dispensed with.

The findings were ultimately issued to the highest ranking civil servants of the provincial government.

- Audit teams were given limited assignments and their findings were collated by senior officers so as to maintain confidentiality of final audit conclusions.
- Records were largely examined at the audit offices and the offices of the investigating agencies.

Audit Findings

- Rupees 6,500 million were drawn over budget authorisation in 6 years by the Animal Husbandry Department.
- During 1993-96, Rupees 4,730 million were drawn by Animal Husbandry Department towards purchase of feed and fodder while approximately only Rupees 100 million was required as per approved scale.
- Just 7 drawing officers of this department, drew approximately Rupees 4,350 million in 3 years even though the total budget provision for the entire department was approximately Rupees 2,300 million. The bulk of the fraudulent payments, amounting to Rupees 4,010 million were made to only 36 suppliers in 6 districts.
- System of centralised selection of vendors for purchase of feed and fodder, was made non-functional. This facilitated issue of purchase orders to little known firms for supply of enormous amounts of feed/fodder, medicines etc.
- Reputed manufacturers and suppliers of medicines were bypassed and established procedures for vendor selection were ignored. Hence medicines were ordered on little known local dealers.
- While Rupees 1,510 million were paid for supply of medicines, hospitals and dispensaries reported receipt of negligible quantities of medicines. They also confirmed

that no indents for medicines had been placed by them. The purchases were therefore fictitious. Numerous discrepancies were noticed in the suppliers invoices and they appeared to be fake.

- Payment authorisation process by the departmental officers and the treasuries violated all prescribed checks and controls. Funds allotment figures, quoted in the bills, were unrealistically high. The treasury officers overlooked this and did not check whether allotments shown actually existed before admitting claims for payments. Several other violations in procedures pointed to the direct complicity of treasury officers in this fraud.

- Finance Department failed to investigate continued excess of expenditures over budget allotments thereby eroding completely the expenditure control mechanisms. This significantly contributed to the unfettered drawl of funds by the Animal Husbandry Department .

- Finance Department overlooked exchequer problems caused due to heavy drawl of funds from treasuries. They did not question or investigate the reasonableness of such cash outgo, even though the Reserve Bank of India periodically kept the department posted regarding cash disbursement from treasuries.

- The Budget Controlling Officer (Director) of the concerned department subverted crucial budgetary and expenditure controls. Instead he provided misleading budgetary forecasts. These were not critically examined in the Finance Department while framing budget estimates of the government.

- Internal check over payments were completely subverted within the Animal Husbandry Department. The bill drawing officers, entrusted with the task of exercising checks, were directly involved in presenting false claims on the basis of fake documents.

- Several officials subsequently found to be involved in the fraud were continued in the same positions in violation of laid-down policy regarding transfer of officials. Some of these officers were also retained in service beyond their dates of superannuation without following laid down procedures for vigilance clearance etc. and in one case despite court orders to the contrary.
- The complicity of top political executives in blocking detailed investigation into the fraudulent drawls and in providing patronage to tainted officials was pointed out in audit and documented.
- Cases of irregular and unauthorised appointment of large number of junior officials were also detected in course of audit examinations.
- An examination of sales tax cases and income tax cases relating to the suppliers who had received fraudulent payments showed that action taken on these by the concerned departments were inadequate and had allowed suppression of taxable sales turnover as well as taxable incomes.

Impact of the Audit

- SAI demonstrated its capability to investigate and report on cases of corruption and fraud even if these involved high level political functionaries.
- Speedy finalisation of audit facilitated the ongoing investigation by the Investigating agencies and commencement of prosecutions against the key officials who were mentioned in the audit report.
- Media coverage of the audit findings created public awareness about the need of improved accountability through the CAG's audit.

- In the light of the audit findings the concerned department and the government could take corrective action for improving financial control.
- Fraud awareness and methodology of audit of fraud related matters in the SAI was developed. This helped in audit of several other cases of fraud in other provincial governments.
- Timely completion of this audit highlighted the importance and usefulness of application of information technology in investigative audit. In the countries where audit records are not computerised, application of sophisticated analytical tools could be possible by creating computerised databases in the audit office, as was demonstrated in this case.

(b) STOCK MARKET FRAUD

It is often said that when the Indian stock markets go through a boom, the whiff of a scam cannot be far behind. But it is not often that the regulator — the Securities and Exchange Board of India (SEBI) in this case — takes action. It is common knowledge that for several years cartels of operators have been cornering shares meant for retail investors in the primary market, referred to as Initial Public Offers (IPO). Often reviled as a "toothless wonder" for failing to protect investors and the integrity of the markets, SEBI issued an Interim Order which was unprecedented in its stringency and stunning in its sweep.

The Interim Order arose out of an investigation, which covered 105 IPOs between February 2003 and November 2005. The 252-page order, while bolstering the findings of a similar (but smaller one in terms of scale and scope) investigation by SEBI reveals shocking details of the fraudulent practices. More significantly, it unearths the complicity of several players who are supposed to perform the role of intermediaries in the market. It reveals how several players managed to open share trading accounts and bank accounts in thousands of fictitious names in order to corner shares issued through IPOs.

An IPO is the first sale of a company's shares to public investors. Typically, it is in the form of an auction sale, a portion of which is reserved for retail investors. Each application for an IPO has to be within a cut-off figure, which makes the applicant eligible for allotment in the retail investors' category. The scam is basically in the illegal cornering of shares meant for retail investors by financiers and market players.

After the advent of paperless trading, made possible by the introduction of demateralised shares, most market-savvy observers claimed that a technology-fix had been found for the widespread malpractices that were rampant in the regime of physical securities trading. One of the significant aspects of the SEBI report is its finding that nearly all sections involved in the regime of paperless trading have played an active part in the scam.

At the apex of the demat trading regime are the two depositories, Central Depository Services (India) Limited (CDSL) and National Securities Depository Limited (NSDL). The next in the link are the Depository Participants (D.P.), which act like banks for investors. Investors have to trade through a D.P. account and each demat account is linked to a bank account.

The most significant finding in the SEBI order relates to the role that D.Ps played in facilitating the scam. Moreover, it found that several leading private banks that are also in the D.P. business aided and abetted the scamsters.

The SEBI order banned two D.Ps from the market. One of them, Hyderabad-based Karvy Stock Broking Ltd., is one of the biggest D.Ps, reportedly serving 22 million investors. Karvy obtained an interim stay from the Andhra Pradesh High Court on May 2, 2005 Pratik D.P. was the other one to be barred by SEBI. In passing the order, G. Anantharaman, whole-time member, SEBI, said that the two D.Ps "*prima facie* do not appear to be fit to deal in securities market as SEBI-registered intermediaries".

Significantly, he also barred several other wings of the Karvy group from their respective areas of operation. The order stated:

"Since the other business groups of Karvy have appeared to have acted in concert in the gamut of the IPO manipulations, I further direct Karvy Stock Broking Ltd., Karvy Computershare Pvt. Ltd., Karvy Investor Services Ltd. and Karvy Consultants Ltd. not to undertake fresh business as a registrar to issue and share transfer agent, excepting those businesses already contracted." The SEBI order, which is also in the nature of a show-cause notice, gave the penalised parties 15 days to explain their position. It also barred 24 "Key Operators" who funnelled the illicitly obtained shares to financiers even before the shares were listed, from trading in the market. Eighty-five financiers who were the ultimate beneficiaries of the scheme were also barred from trading in the market. Twelve D.Ps, including those aligned to private banks such as the Centurion Bank, HDFC Bank, ING Vysya Bank and IDBI, were prohibited from opening fresh demat accounts "until further notice".

Soon after the order was issued on the night of April 27, 2005 Indiabulls Securities, one of the 85 ordered to stay out of the market for its role as a financier, moved SEBI officials for a review of the order. The fact that SEBI amended its order soon after the markets opened the following day has been cited as evidence of the pressure that is being mounted on SEBI. On May 4, 2005 the Gujarat High Court stayed SEBI's order barring Saumil A. Bhavnagari, one of the 85 financiers named in the interim order.

Despite the criticism that it has bungled as a regulator, there is no doubt that it was SEBI which first investigated the IPO scam. In late 2005 the Income Tax Department found that an investor in Ahmedabad had 5,000 demat accounts in his name. Later, in February 2006, the Central Bureau of Investigation (CBI) found that one of the Key Operators (or "Master Account Holders"), Ahmedabad-based Roopalben Panchal had issued advertisements offering to photograph people free of cost. The CBI found that she used these photographs to go with fictitious names for opening bank and demat accounts for investment in demat accounts.

SEBI had asked the stock exchanges to report suspicious off-market sales of shares soon after allotment but before listing. SEBI received the reports from the stock markets in October 2005, which indicated "large-scale off-market transactions" prior to the listing of the shares.

SEBI noticed "a large number of multiple dematerialised accounts with common addresses". SEBI passed an interim order restraining such account holders from participating in all future IPOs. It also directed the depositories to freeze effectively these dematerialised accounts. Soon after this, in January, 2006 SEBI passed another Interim Order based on its investigation of another major IPO, that of the IDFC (earlier Infrastructure Development Finance Corporation). It found that "the very same players" played a similar role in this case too.

The SEBI investigation reveals three significant actors in the IPO scam — financiers, "Key Operators" and thousands of *benami* applicants who filed thousands of IPO applications (afferent accounts in SEBI parlance). The financier was the lynchpin in the entire operation and also the ultimate beneficiary of the scheme. The Key Operator's primary function was to act as a funnel to consolidate the successful allotments of the *benami* applicants. The audit trail, investigated by SEBI, shows that in most cases they also provided finance to the Key Operators for making the applications for the IPO. The investigation also found that the financiers sold the allotments that they purchased "off-market" soon after allotment from the Key Operators for a premium upon listing. SEBI found that the Key Operators "allowed their demat accounts for temporarily parking credits received from *benami* applicants before transferring them to the financiers". The *benami* demat account holders constituted the last leg in this sordid scheme. The successful applicants transferred their allotments to the Key Operators before the shares were listed, in off-market transactions.

Since multiple demat accounts does not constitute an abnormality, for the purpose of the investigation SEBI determined that entities that gained from transactions involving the off-market sale from 500 or more accounts were those of Key Operators.

SEBI found that the 24 Key Operators it had identified had resorted to "abusive practices" in 21 of the 105 IPOs it investigated. It also found that a total of 58,938 fictitious accounts had been used for cornering the retail portion of the IPO. Nearly 85 per cent of these accounts were held with Karvy DP. For instance, Roopalben Panchal used 81,708 demat accounts for applying to 16 IPOs during the period covered by the SEBI investigation. All the demat accounts were with Karvy Stock Broking. An overwhelming proportion of these accounts were solely meant for applying for IPOs. For example, of the 7,751 accounts that were opened on August 16, 2004, only 15 remained active when SEBI conducted its investigation. Many of these belonged to Roopalben.

It found that many of these accounts had been opened on a few dates close to the date of the IPO. Moreover, the addresses of these demat account holders were the same as those of the Key Operators identified by SEBI. Significantly, 14 of the 24 Key Operators had their demat accounts with Karvy DP. The order observed that while Karvy DP was "actively in league" by opening demat accounts for many of the Key Operators, it also served as a conduit for the bulk of the *benami* demat account holders. Anantharaman pointed out that "the numbers are too significant to be dismissed as normal incidence of business".

SEBI has also castigated the banks that facilitated these illicit transactions. For instance, it found "numerous irregularities and non-adherence to Know Your Client norms". It observed that the fact that 286 savings bank accounts were opened by one of the Key Operators with HDFC's D.P. operations is "clearly proof enough for the plan to open multiple demat accounts to channel the funds in a manner that would bury the audit trail".

In the wake of the IPO scam there have been suggestions that banks should stay at arm's length from D.P. operations. There is commendable reason why the two need to be separated by a safe distance. The relationship between an investor and a D.P. is basically a contract between two private parties. The D.P., without actually having access to the shares of its client, acts as a custodian of the shares in demat form.

Banks, however, are in a completely different league. Their fiduciary responsibilities extend beyond their immediate clients because they raise deposits from a larger customer base. The ease with which private banks are able to mix fee-based D.P. activities with their banking operations thus appears to be dangerous for the health of the financial system.

The depositories have also drawn flak in the order. Anantharaman has pointed out that there were "contributory lapses" on the part of NSDL, which accounts for 80 per cent of the depositor business. SEBI found that the depository had used "dummy numbers" in its databases, particularly for dates prior to April 1999. It also found instances of "junk data".

SEBI's critics have said that it has bungled by acting hastily. In particular, they fault SEBI for passing an ex parte order. However, SEBI's action has drawn praise from those who feel that the regulator has not acted decisively in the past. Perhaps the most significant revelation is that the entire IPO process is riddled with lacunae. The SEBI report reveals that intermediaries along the chain, including registrars and transfer agents of the issues, depositories, depository participants, merchant bankers and banks, have played a part in the scandal. It would be a pity if SEBI's painstaking work is reduced to a matter of keeping a few shady operators at bay. Much more - the very health of the financial system — is at stake.

(c) SATYAM SCAM

The shocking confession by B. Ramalinga Raju, Satyam Computer Services erstwhile chairman, about years of accounting chicanery by the software firm is reason enough for the government to step in and take action. The centre invoked the power bestowed on it by the Companies Act, 1956 and moved the Company Law Board immediately to appoint new directors to the board to protect the interest of all the stakeholders-investors, employees, clients and debtors. Such a measure assumes urgency as Satyam, which employs more than 50,000 people and services more than 650 clients across the globe, needs to continue as a going concern. A vacuum at the top would be demoralizing, and government action alone at this stage may reassure employees and clients. Further, given the gravity of the problem, the government along with the regulators such as the Securities and Exchange Board of India (SEBI) and the Institute of Chartered Accountants of India (ICAI) must thoroughly investigate the affairs of the company. Books of accounts of the previous years need to be meticulously examined and the management questioned to gauge the extent of the fraud, and everyone responsible for the fraud as well as those who abetted it must be prosecuted. The unfolding of events also point to the failure of the audit firm Price Waterhouse, very obviously they did not verify the assets or ask enough questions. How else would the company have overstated assets over the years to the extent almost Rs 7000 crore, including cash and bank balance of Rs. 5040 crore? The ICAI, as the regulator for accountants and auditors, needs to seek answers from the firm and take disciplinary action against members who failed in their duty. After all, like independent director, auditors too have fiduciary duties towards all stakeholders.

Given the extent of fraud and likelihood of lawsuits worth billions of dollar, Satyam is unlikely to find a suitor anytime soon. The only thing going for the company at this stage is that employees and clients cannot move en masse to competitors. So, the interim administrators of the company, together with its major shareholders, put their heads together to chart out the best course for survival.

The fraud at Satyam may lead to one of the largest directors and officer insurance claims in India. The company has a $75 million cover to defend directors who are under fire for dereliction of duty, from legal action in India and abroad.

D & O covers compensate a company and its directors for the cost of defending itself against legal actions. Although the terms of Satyam's D & O cover are not known, such policies can have the coverage extended to cover payments towards damages, judgments and settlements. These policies are almost mandatory for companies going for a US listing. According to insurance officials, the minimum cost of defence in the US is around \$5-\$6 million and expenses soar in the event of class action suit.

Besides international listings, expatriate directors have been the drivers for D & O policies with some insisting on a D & O cover before joining the board. The cover gains significance because corporate laws do not allow a company to pay for the defense of directors. The D & O cover was acquired by Satyam from Tata AIG for a primary amount, beyond which insurers like New India Assurance and ICICI Lombard General Insurance step in. Senior officials at New India and ICICI Lombard confirmed their participation at higher levels of the cover.

According to Praveen Vashishta, MD of Howden Insurance Brokers – a firm which specializes in D & O policies – the Satyam incident would lead independent directors to actually question whether they are covered. Some insurers fear that just as D & O covers became more expensive in the fallout of the Enron fraud in the US, insurers may get wary about the Indian market. However, Mr. Vashishta said "I don't think there would be much of an impact on pricing as this is a one off case and there is enough capacity in the market."

Unlike property insurance, D & O liability cover is sold in layers with primary insurer underwriting the first layer. According to industry officials, Tata AIG's presence as a primary reinsurer would be reassuring to directors since AIG is very strong in these policies in the reinsurance market. Earlier, the most publicized D & O claim was the settlement between Infosys and an ex-employee who had filed harassment charges against the Infosys' US head. The claim had ended with a $3 million out of the court settlement.

The arrest and judicial remand of Ramalinga Raju, his brother and the Chief Financial Officer of the Satyam Computer Services Limited might be the start of an effective legal process to bring to justice the self-confessed perpetrator of the biggest corporate fraud in Indian history. However, the latest developments cannot obscure the inordinate delay on the part of the Andhra Pradesh government in setting the law in motion and going after those who have committed grave cognisable offences that have an international dimension. Journalists, legal experts, investors, and politicians have raised the question why it took almost two-and-a-half days for the State police to act after the main perpetrator incriminated himself (even if, as some experts suggest, his defence lies in his self-incrimination). In crimes of this nature and magnitude, it is essential that the investigating agencies move swiftly to collect the evidence before anyone has a chance to tamper with it and to demonstrate (as high-minded jurists tend to say) that 'howsoever high you maybe, the law is above you.' The explanation that the State police were hampered by the absence of a formal complaint does not wash. After all, the offences admitted were cognisable under the Indian Penal Code.

In contrast to the State governments procrastination in setting the ordinary criminal law in motion, the Union Ministry of Corporate Affairs as well as the captial, market regulator, the Securities and Exchange Board of India (SEBI) have acted with due speed in far more complicated areas. Coordination between these agencies and the investigating State police will be critical in this case. Going by Mr. Raju's own confession, he and the other perpetrators can be prosecuted under the Companies Act, the Securities Contracts (Regulation) Act, the SEBI Act, and the Indian Penal Code. Given the magnitude of the scam, the Central Bureau of Investigation was brought in. However, it must be remembered that cases such as the Satyam scam have dragged on for years in the courts. Neither specific legal provision nor the specialised prosecuting agencies have really helped in speeding up the process. Although not strictly comparable, the Harshad Mehta-led stock market scam attracted the legal processes, including the setting up of a special court at Mumbai. More than 15 years after the first case was filed, the special court finds itself bogged down in the scam cases. Many of the accused, including the principal perpetrator, are dead.

Is the Satyam scandal just about a promoter manipulating the financial statements of his company to show a superior performance? Or is it about systematic siphoning of funds from the company over the years? Emerging events seem to increasingly point to the latter.

Let's start with the so-called "confession statement" of Mr Ramalinga Raju, the disgraced chairman of the company. Lawyers have already expressed doubts over whether the statement can actually be deemed a confession and enough to implicate Mr Raju. Indeed, they say that it is a very well drafted document designed to draw attention to the hole in the finances without implicating himself anywhere for any act of commission. A careful reading of the statement shows that there is indeed merit in this view. Mr Raju has pointed to cash balances not being the same as reported in the audited financial statements, he has said of how revenues were inflated, and so on. But nowhere has he said that he was responsible for this nor has he pointed his finger at anyone else. Of course, as the chairman, the buck stops with him but that is not the same as saying "I did it". If anything, he has tried to project himself as the saviour by pointing out how he arranged Rs 1230 crore for the company and how neither he nor the managing director "took even one rupee/dollar from the company and have not benefited in financial terms on account of the inflated results".

Mr Raju appears to have attempted to deflect attention from what is possibly the more serious crime of siphoning of funds to the relatively lesser one of accounting skulduggery. This is being clever by half. How on earth did he think that the shareholders, lenders, legal agencies and the world at large would believe him on this?

People who were and are working in responsible positions in Satyam say that the company has a real business going and some of its divisions are extremely profitable and there is no question of doubting the revenues from them. There is no way that operating margin will be as low as 3 per cent, they say, unless of course, if money had been sucked out of the company.

The second event that raises doubts is the carefully orchestrated arrest of Mr Raju. He surrendered himself to the police the night before he was to appear before the SEBI investigating team. The arrest and remand ensured that SEBI was unable to interrogate him.

The market regulator will eventually be able to quiz him, but the question is: Will there be evidence destroyed before that? As it is, there is the possibility that Mr Raju may have destroyed crucial evidence implicating him before he went public with his "confession". And then, there is the political angle to the scandal. Mr Raju and his companies (Maytas group) have been beneficiaries of large public contracts for transport systems and irrigation project in Andra Pradesh.

We must take right lessons from the Satyam Saga. Satyam is one of the leading software companies of India—the so-called 'Enron' of India. Satyam and its inverse 'Maytas' the apparent failings of the Audit procedures of PW—all these now-a-days have become a common topic of discussion. 'Greed' appears to be the main driving force causing several corporate failures both in India and overseas. Money belonging to the company invariably diverted to other projects undertaken by the same group and manipulation of the share prices in the listed companies prior to accruing the domestic or overseas capital market. In Satyam's case also, in the eventuality of its ever being made public, it may be discovered that money has been diverted to the previously booming, real estate market to encash, make personal windfall projects and then reverse the manipulation. In the boom period the manipulation has failed to imagine about risk of down turn. It appears that in Satyam case the Audit have failed with statutory requirement of reconciling cash and bank balances with the bank. These days it is very common to receive Bank statement including fixed deposit receipt stating: "This is a computer generated statement and hence does not require signature'. Internal knowhow is to generate its own system. Bank statements, receipt or confirmation may be a cause of failure of Audit procedures. In corporate inventory manipulation inflated figures of finish goods stock etc. is commonly done to obtain loan from Banks or raise their credit limit. BIFR is flooded with many financially sick corporate.

In the boom time of the capital market the management is under pressure to perform. There is immediate pressure to enter the capital market at unrealistic valuation as free pricing is permitted under SEBI guidelines. Modern management boys' mantras of doing valuation is only to attract attention to the capital market by raising earning per share and the earning before interest depreciation taxation and amortization. Standard method of valuation and risk factor devised by experts have now been forgotten and not found to be followed in many of the companies. Market capitalization became a major area of concern even for corporate who did not wish to access the capital market. Top and bottom lines had to be even at the cost of paying income tax and dividends on nonexistent profits and reserve. Existing manipulations to satisfy the capital market, the compounding problems of losses on account of derivatives and future position, the obligations on unlisted companies into which PE investments have flowed to list besides dealings with the beleaguered West and Japan which may lead to stuck receivable, will all result increasing the risk of corporate defaults in meeting obligation to lenders. Audit committee must focus on the companies investment portfolio including debt and enquity security. To identify declines in value or impairments that should be reflected in the financials. One has come across instances where statutory auditors have been the de facto internal auditors as well, though professional ethics prohibits.

The malady affecting the corporate can be cured only by better quality implementation and compliance. Free pricing of shares must be tagged with ethics of honest reporting. Banks have to be more alert and closely monitor the corporate performance. Market analysts and financial professionals alongwith Auditors must be ethical not only in their actions but should reflect in their action also at the social level.

Government has now decided to make all of the top executives and board members of Satyam Computer Services including the independent director, answerable for the fraud perpetuated within the company. A director reliance on the co-directors and other officers cannot be unquestioning. He too is duty hound to ensure that sufficient controls are in place so that abuses can be quickly identified.

SATYAM TAKEOVER BY TECH-MAHINDRA

Mahindras are shrewd businessmen and know what they are getting into. Hestor Liang of United Biscuits once said, "Buildings age become dilapidated, machines wear out, car rust, people die, but what lives on are brands." Tech-Mahindra has taken over Satyam in a competitive bid, defeating the L&T, which had forked out a small sum of Rs 2889/- crore to gain a controlling 51 per cent equity in the company whose troubles started with Ramalinga Raju confessions. The deal might benefit Satyam, as it immediately catapults the combined entity into the elite stable of Indian Software. Though the Mahindras are not dominant players in the technology space (they are in telecom space in technology), they are most certainly a respected name in the Indian industry, with a track record of success in business and acknowledge ability to launch successful brands across categories. The troubled Satyam brand will also benefit from solidity that the mere name implies and the consistency in management of Mahindras. In Satyam deal they followed a certain process and obtained the help of independent directors. Deepak Parekh is one of the independent directors, though he absented himself from the Board meeting in which the modus operandi of take over of Satyam was discussed. The senior management of M&M and Tech Mahindra first got together to look at Satyam. They then came out with a business plan on potential challenges, opportunities etc. This was followed by a presentation to the M&M Board 5-6 days before the bid. The boards of M&M and Tech Mahindra were led by independent directors of the 12-member M&M board, out of which eight are independent directors, which meant all the discussions were led and guided by them. There was a complete convergence of views between the two boards. The decision to bid was taken after that. They were aware that like any other business opportunity, Satyam also has its own set of risks. There were a whole lot of uncertainties around Satyam. The class action suits in U.S. were a big area of uncertainties. But history of some class action suits indicate the settlement had taken place at 5 cents/10 cents per dollar over the years. There was another risk of Satyam balance sheet. But overall it was a great company with good reputation, with its clients coupled with an excellent workforce. What has happened was very unfortunate. Ramalinga Raju had built a great company. Tech Mahindra has its own ability, it raised Rs 25000/- crore on its own. After take over, chairman of Tech Mahindra has said, "We have taken a calculated risk in making this bid. We will make it work." He also called this acquisition a "game changer" as it gives the company much needed diversification.

With the news of take over by Mahindras, the 53000 beleaguered employees were much relieved. It was an achievement for Indian

Business globally, that the newly constituted board of Satyam got its act together and the interest of the corporate world in a brand which had come under the cloud. The word Satyam is related to truth whereas the company has certainly stood for everything except truth which is antonyms of Satyam. What happened in Satyam was that it was a huge scandal. Nobody could stand up and say what was happening was wrong. Even those who thought what was happening was wrong did not have the courage and were not in a position to say it was wrong. Any community that encourages directly or indirectly, a feudal structure or dictatorship is bound to result in disaster. On the other hand any community or company that espouses the cause of democracy committed with fair, balanced transparency and accountability will never see a disaster. Serious Fraud Investigation Officer (SFIO), after its three months probe has told the Government that Ramalinga Raju and family systematically offloaded their stakes in the company while artificially inflating the stock price with imaginary profits and brand-building efforts. To maintain the high share price, Satyam depicted a healthy picture of the company year after year by inflating sales and current asset figures. The manipulations were done to maintain competitive financial ratio vis-a-vis rivals in the software services industry. Satyam spent a huge amount of money on brand building and procurement of ERP packages such as SAP, even though they were not able to fully utilize the existing Oracle Financial Package. The huge investments were shown to gain confidence of analysts as wells as the investors that a large amount of cash and bank balance were being used for prudent business practices. To meet the expectations of the investors, they made major acquisitions from time to time which ultimately proved to be losing propositions, by falsifying the accounts for several years and through reckless spending just to project the company cash-rich, the promoters had brought the entity to a stage of bankruptcy. Raju's family members offloaded individual holding in Satyam through three associate companies and other individuals instead of selling them directly in the open market. Hit by the global economic crisis in Sept 2008, they failed to meet the margin calls. As a result, Satyam had to pledge 3.61 crore additional shares of Maytas Infra.

There is still a lot of uncertainty around the restatement of accounts, legal liabilities, transition plans and surplus employees. The sale to a strategic investor, in that sense, is not an end in itself. It is a promising start. Even though the game-changing buyout has the ability to free Tech Mahindra from the overwhelming dependence on one client (British Telecom) and one vertical, (telecom), it comes straddled with its set of challenges.

Thanks to the way Satyam has been handled, it has the potential to become a classic case study on how to manage the after-effect of such deep and massive corporate shocks. In probably similar incident in case of ENRON of USA, the Government failed to take immediate measures to bail out the company. The entire episode in Satyam case has demonstrated India's ability to handle large crisis, an ability that not many people have thought existed. A key takeaway from the incident is clearly the finesse with which it was handled. Education and ethos within corporate India is important and the acceptability level is required to be changed. Tougher stance is required for ethos and self discipline. The sale of 51 per cent stake was conducted under the watchful eye of former Chief Justice of India, Mr S P Bharucha. The Board decided to conduct the initial round through sealed financial bids. Without a floor price, holding an open auction in the first round could have proved fatal. The strategy paid off when the Board received the highest bid from Tech Mahindra at Rs 58 a share and such the process was completed. The secretary in the ministry of corporate affairs Anurag Goel was at the helm of the officialdom that managed the whole process of saving the high quality company by separating it from the consequences of the fraud. It was an effective partnership that was forged between the industry and the regulatory authorities worked well and made this happen. The Government at various levels acted in tandem with a remarkable degree of decisiveness and swiftness. Both had a common cause and they jointly worked for it. They have been able to use the existing legal framework in an innovative way, perhaps in a way it has never been used earlier. The concern was the interest of shareholders, large number of employees and the clients as these people have not done any wrong. The Government saw the issue as much larger than that of an individual company and was right from start aware of the possible implications of its action.

The Board members appointed by the Government were from diverse fields. Each of them was instrumental in carrying the process through.

Change of brand name of Satyam may be helpful but it will be difficult to remove the old image of Satyam from its existing employees and most of its customers. They will have to constantly demonstrate that they are "new and improved" in every aspect of their customer service and delivery. Every success of the new venture will hinge on this important difference. The company should resist the temptation to talk to an ever eager media and focus internally on its most important target. The company is required to focus on retaining talent as that will be crucial in ensuring stability for its customers, who have stood by it during turbulent times. Communication of stability and a reassurance to existing employees will have to be punctuated with a clear articulation of a new set of values and a new direction that will be the basis of the company's functioning. Also, riding on Satyam will mean trading on unfamiliar ground, both in terms of geography and verticals. Given that Tech Mahindra has only 25429 employees, the acquisition of a company bigger than itself may have its own challenges. While a combined employee strength of 73429 may make Tech Mahindra next only to India's third largest I T services provider Wipro, managing the integration may not be easy.

The new management have decided to firm up a cost cutting plan that could cover rationalisation of employees. The audit committee, Deolite and KMPG comprising of government nominee on Satyam board will also take stock of the progress on the restatement of the account of the scandal hit IT firm. The new management, Tech Mahindra reckons that the company has an excess staff of around 10,000 in total of 41,622 staffs. The rationalisation exercise may target employees who have not been billed for over six months now. They may be offered 40% of their existing salary for six months, but may eventually have to leave the firm as they are considered as non-productive as they do not bring any revenue to the firm. Lay-off plans may be discussed as part of the cost cutting measures.

Satyam revenue has decreased as their business has been adversely affected since the fraud has been detected. Legal liabilities and acquisition related disputes mounted after their director confession. On 9th June '09 Satyam disclosed its revenue and profit figure for the quarter ended Dec '08, January and February '09 with a disclaimer saying the information had not been audited/examined by the independent auditor, the actual figures may vary. But investors cheered the stock as the firm reported revenue of Rs 2000/- crores and surprise profit of Rs 181 crores for the Dec '08 quarter. Now the shareholders will be able to tender their shares in an open offer. Tech Mahindra will also be able to get the required 20% share from the open offer otherwise preferential allotment to take its total holding in Satyam to 51% will be made and they will be again a winner in second round of preferential issue of shares inasmuch as it is doubtful that there will be many takers for the open offer of Satyam.

Cost-Cutting Satyam Through Virtual Pool

Satyam board headed by Kiran Karnik, a Govt appointed nominee, to bail out the fraud-hit company, before his stepping down had unveiled a plan which would see it sidestep the sensitive issue of sacking staff but helped save large sums of money in salaries. The new scheme called as "Virtual Pool" came just a day ahead of the commencement of an open offer by Tech Mahindra for an additional 20% stake. The plan to cut staff cost appeared to have received political blessings. The chief minister had recommended that employees who may be finally retrenched should get a suitable compensation package. Whereas some employees of Satyam were unimpressed, believing that the "virtual pool" is just another way of handing out pink slips of a very light shade. It may turn out a politically acceptable way of doing lay-off.

The virtual pool scheme in brief is that, about one fourth of staff, (10,000) was allowed to join the scheme by taking time off from work on sharply reduced pay for up to six months starting the third weak of June '09. The plan expected to save Rs one crore per day. Staff costs accounted for more than half of the company expenses. Employees who had not been part of revenue earnings assignments for at least the past three months, including support staff were expected to join the virtual pool scheme. Such non-bailable resources employees counted around 14,000. The employees got 40-45% of their current salary, including medical, insurance and provident fund benefits. The scheme was required to be reviewed every six months. Employment status of staff remained the same in virtual pool scheme.

A virtual pool is a tried and tested practice among the multinational companies. Many employees who do not want to lose jobs in premium companies are happy with such offers. This is good move combined to meet challenges in a business cycle and mitigate human pain. Most IT companies are looking at ways to cope with surplus staff and reckon this is an innovative way of retaining the excellent human assets despite the difficult global economic condition and to ensure the company financially viable.

CHAPTER 2 TAX EVASION CASES

TAX EVASION THREAT TO DEVELOPMENT

The global economic slowdown will hit the poorest nations hardest. Demand for their exports is falling. Prices of raw materials are plunging. Flows of money from migrant workers to families back home will shrink as unemployment rises elsewhere. In these circumstances it is more important than ever that rich countries deliver on aid promises. That is why the Oil Exporting Countries Donors (OECD) have called on the world's main donors to join an Aid Pledge to stick by their commitments. As world leaders head to Doha for a U.N. meeting on financing for development on November 29, 2008, however, another dimension of the issue needs urgent attention: tax systems. Efficient tax systems underpin development. Rich countries rely on taxes to finance aid flows. In developing countries, locally generated taxes are a much bigger source of development finance than aid. Effective tax systems, based on cooperative relationships between governments, businesses and individuals, are a bedrock for democracy and growth. When businesses and citizens form part of the formal economy, good tax administration can provide for pensions, social security payments and other instruments of the modem State. But there's a dark side. Tax dodgers in developed and developing countries deprive governments of revenues. Many of them take advantage of the lack of transparency in tax havens. Developing countries are estimated to lose to tax havens almost three times what they get from developed countries in aid. If taxes on assets hidden by tax dodgers were collected in their owners' jurisdictions, billions of dollars could become available for financing development,

Fighting tax evasion calls for cooperation between developed and developing countries. At home governments must enact fair and effective policies and make it easy for taxpayers to comply with their obligations. Internationally, they must push for greater transparency in cross-border financial transactions. Ties with Commonwealth countries and dependencies that operate as offshore financial centres make it uniquely well placed to push for improved standards of transparency. At the same time, it can give a lead in helping developing countries improve their tax administration. We need to be realistic. Developing countries often lack the resources to build effective tax systems. Citizen may be unwilling to pay on the grounds that governments misuse the funds. It can be difficult to implement fair taxation in low-income, agrarian economies. And the poor are often subject to an equivalent of tax, in bribes and informal fees.

But something can be done. The OECD's decade-long drive against tax havens and evasion is bearing fruit in the form of bilateral treaties aimed at improving transparency and exchange of information. The trend is spreading beyond the OECD, with China and South Africa joining this campaign. At the same time, donor countries are helping poorer nations develop fair tax services.

Significantly, developing countries are joining forces too. An African Tax Administration Forum is being developed under the leadership of Botswana, Cameroon, Ghana, Nigeria Rwanda, South Africa and Uganda. By inviting governments to share good practices, it aims to improve service delivery and taxpayer education. Success will increase accountability, strengthen democracy and combat corruption. In 2006, only $88m of a total $103bn in official development assistance from OECD countries was dedicated to tax-related tasks. But aid targeted at capacity building in revenue administrations is money well spent. Donor support to the Rwanda Revenue Authority brought a dramatic increase in tax revenue, from 9 per cent of GDP in 1998 to 14.7 per cent in 2005, with an equally significant effect on state accountability. The last time when we faced a major global downturn, aid budgets fell dramatically — curtailing investment in agriculture, infrastructure, social welfare and political stability. Similar cuts now would be even more damaging, after volatility in commodity prices and a global food crisis have already hit the poor. Cuts may bring short-term savings to donor governments, but they would cost much more in the longer term in extra spending on security and humanitarian aid.

Earlier, OECD donors joined in an Aid Pledge to maintain aid flows consistent with promises at Gleneagles and elsewhere. If combined with a joint effort to fight tax evasion, the results for development could be significant. The OECD, as the leading international organisation with a mandate to work on tax policy, is committed to this objective. More effective tax systems in developed and developing countries would help to build a stronger, cleaner and fairer world economy. And they would help the poorest the most.

Golden Decision

The period commencing from 1991 to 1998 was perhaps one of the best in the Finance Ministry, including the Revenue Department. The only setback for the department was Mumbai blast case, where some custom officials were found to be allegedly involved in the conspiracy to smuggle explosives that were later used to trigger off the serial blast in Mumbai city. This was a period of great excitement and expectation all around as one new measure followed the other every now and then. To appreciate the true import of the new measures, one has to take into account the difficult circumstances in which they were initiated. The economic condition of the country at that time was rather precarious. Bold reform measures were taken since any failure would have meant disaster for the economy with every possibility of a reversion to the era of high tariffs and controls. Experts defined these reforms as structural changes, healthy growth of GDP rates etc. Economic reforms reduced the burden of both the direct and indirect taxes, licences, controls and restrictions gave away, procedures were simplified and there was greater transparency in the administration. There was unprecedented growth in revenue over the preceding year. Export made quantum leaps and world recognized these developments.

One such specific measure was allowance of import of gold in the year 1991. Despite some initial hiccups the scheme was successful and gave a body blow to gold smuggling which had bedeviled our economy since independence. Preventive measures taken till then couid at best keep this menace under some check but failed to eliminate it. Some bold economic solution was required. One cannot appreciate how momentous this decision was without comprehending the enormity of the problem of gold smuggling. It dwarfed all other economic offences. It was the nucleus of the parallel economy of black money and gave rise to and got sustenance from such activities as hawala, under and over invoicing, drug trafficking, evasion of various taxes and numerous import and export frauds. Ironically India having half of its population under poverty line has been one of the largest consumers of gold ahead of the riches countries of the world. Compared to its requirements the quantity of gold that is produced from mines in India is infinitesimal. About 25 to 30 percent of its requirements was met by recycling old gold within the country. The rest had to come from outside. As its import was prohibited the demand had to be met by smuggling. In the year 2000-01, India had imported 571 tons of gold. The quantity of imports has been constantly growing up thereafter. In the year 1991-92 just before the import of gold was allowed the quantity of gold was approximately from 300 to 400 tons. With the new policy, smuggling of gold was replaced by regular imports thus contributing to the economy in a positive manner and economic crime came to an end to a larger extent.

Another such bold measure was lowering of customs and central excise duties, at that time amongst the highest in the world. This principle yielded positive result and the measure succeeded by showing a tremendous growth.

CENTRAL EXCISE EVASION CASES

Some of the manufacturers evade central excise duty by adopting a noble modus operandi, sometimes they are not caught but what I have seen in my career of more than two decades that lastly they definitely come in the grip of the law. It is rightly said that illegal earnings never bear good fruits. People in India by and large appear to be permissive about economic offences, however big they might be. The reason is that their impact is remote and indirect. The majority of people who evade taxes have no qualms about it. But their dimension and sweep is such that they are always a threat to legislative system. Above all, they are a blatant breach of the immense trust now placed on public, by way of removal of restrictions, licences, controls and checks, simplification of procedures and reduction of rates of taxes and duties, which have opened up immense possibilities for legitimate trade. Any breach, therefore justifies a more serious view and stricter action. Generally we miss this nowadays. If there are some who enforce these laws strictly, as these laws should be, they are quite often called as 'rigid' or 'inflexible'. There are some honest manufacturers who never intend to evade central excise duty. Sometimes, a caucus of employes is formed comprising of employees involved in production and marketing alongwith departmental officers jointly evade Central Excise duty and share the illegal earnings. Central Excise levy is the basic levy from which Sale Tax on sales of goods and Income Tax on income of sale of goods is levied. Thus if a manufacturer evades Central Excise duty, he is also further evading Sales Tax and Income Tax.

Some of such modus operandi, I will like to discuss in brief without disclosing their identity :-

1. M/s 'X' Ltd., a reputed manufacturer of cement was caught red handed in evasion of Central Excise duty to the tune of more than Rs. 5 crores by adopting the following modus operandi:

   (a) Their factory was situated near mines of Lime Stone. Lime Stone being one of the major raw material used in the manufacture of cement. They used to submit monthly statement in respect of total quantity of Lime Stone excavated from quarry to the Mining Department. But during search of their office in mines some lorry receipts were found indicating transport of excavated Lime Stone to their factory. On interrogation of the Driver and owner of the trucks it was learnt that they used to carry more quantity of Lime Stone in their trucks than the prescribed limit of 10MT to the factory from mines but L/Rs were prepared of 10Mt. only and on record payments were made for the differential quantity they used to receive payments in cash.

   (b) On further investigation it was also learnt that once goods train carrying clinker (an intermediate product) to their sister concerns met an accident and the accident investigation team of the Railway had given their findings that due to overweight of wagons the accident occurred. The said factory used to regularly send clinker to their sister concerns. The findings of the Railway Enquiry Committee later served as an important evidence.

   (c) Further it was found that excess cement manufactured out of excess Lime Stone was sold in used bags purchased from *kabadi* (Scrap Dealer) who used to sell these jute cement bags. Account of such bags was never disclosed to the department.

(d) On collection of such evidences a case was registered. Party had obtained caveat from the High Court. Later on the Hon'ble High Court decided the case in favour of the department and held that let the first case be decided by the department. Furthermore, taking the shelter of the Natural Justice, party requested for change of adjudicating officer. The case was confirmed by another adjudicating officer. By that time there was 'Kar Vivad Samadhan Scheme' and party opted for the scheme and deposited duty and saved itself form imposition of penalty and prosecution.

2. M/s X Pvt Ltd, a well established Handmade Biri manufacturing unit having more than 50 branches all over India, was once caught evading central excise duty on their product . Tobacco is the principal raw material used in the manufacture of Biri . There is a fixed ratio/formula of tobacco used by each manufacturer for their product separately, required to be disclosed to the department at the starting of the unit. The manufacturer had made a central warehouse secretly from where they used to distribute tobacco to their different branches for manufacture of Biri which were clandestinely removed without payment of duty. Once on a surprise visit and verification to the unit, tobacco was found short, their final product stock was also found short than recorded balance indicating clandestine removal. Prima-facie case was registered. On further investigation it was also learnt that the manager of the factory sells the best quality tobacco to the local manufacturers on premium price and sometimes forgets to adjust the quantity from the tobacco received unaccounted from the central warehouse. More evidences were collected from their other branches in

this regard and it was conclusively established that tobacco stored in the undisclosed central warehouse was being used in manufacture of Biri which were being removed without payment of duty. The case was decided against the party on first adjudication. Party went in appeal, at first appeal the case was also confirmed. On second appeal, the Tribunal remanded the case back for de-novo adjudication on the ground that cross examination of detecting officers was not allowed by the adjudicating officer. In Central Excise adjudication is a quasi judicial proceedings and it is not necessarily based on the facts of the case to allow cross examination while adjudicating the case on merits. However obeying the orders of the Appellate Authority the case was re-adjudicated after allowing the cross examination of the detecting officers. By that time one officer was retired and died, he was not cross examined. In cross examination Supreme Court Lawyers were called and brought in a chartered Plane. The evidences were very strong and the lawyers could not overcome the officers in cross examinations. The case was again confirmed on de-novo adjudication. Prosecution was also launched in the economic offence court and in the court also, it was confirmed. On second appeal in the Tribunal and High Court, appeal of the party was allowed. In the whole process, it took almost more than 20 years.

3. During Audit of one PVC Pipe Manufacturing company, one duplicate set of invoices was noticed. On further investigation from their customers in the market during survey it was found that they have sold PVC Pipes of their brand on duplicate set of invoice which when compared with that of mentioned in the monthly return was not found to be tallied. The purchaser on interrogation stated that they have also paid the amount to them. On search of their premises some related incriminating

documents/records were found and seized as an evidence. After discrete interrogation the proprietor of the unit accepted and paid the duty. But due to legal constraints duty of the last five years only could be collected and got deposited.

4. One floor/Wall Tiles manufacturing unit was engaged in evasion of Central Excise duty by clandestinely removing more boxes of tiles than recorded in their invoices. The extra packets used to be transported on top of the driver's cabin in truck, where generally no one goes for checking during verification. The whole stock of the unit was got physically verified under proper Panchnama. In each and every stages Panchnama was drawn before the witnesses to ensure clear transparency in the verification and counting in the case. The case was confirmed and the party appeal was dismissed. It was learnt that the production and marketing staff of the unit were engaged in this malpractice without the knowledge of the owner. They were removed from the company. The owner lastly sold the unit.

5. There is a scheme of exemption from Central Excise duty to the manufacturers who have set up their manufacturing units for development of undeveloped areas of North-East, Jammu & Kashmir, Uttrakhand, Himachal Pradesh etc. The aim of the scheme is to encourage setting up of new industries in the undeveloped area to enhance the economic growth and promote employment to the residents of that area. Some cases have been detected where unit was on paper only and found to have been enjoying the undue benefit.

These days a tendency has developed that when a scheme of development of undeveloped area is announced by the government, the opportunist manufacturer come and establish their unit and avail the concessional benefits like land at very low price, power at reduced rate, deferred payment of sales tax etc.

They procure loan from banks on easy terms and condition. But after lapse of the concessional scheme, say 5-10 years they declare their unit sick and leave the place after securing their profit, without paying the bank loan, taxes arrears. In many cases of the Bureau of Industrial and Financial Reconstruction (BIFR), the proceedings used to go on interminably. When BIFR was conceived in the decades of seventies, it was meant to provide a swift assessment by an expert group to see whether a loss making enterprise was capable of turning around or not. If it was capable, a revival package was announced to evolve the unit, if it was not, the unit was to be wound up. This was the noble aim of the BIFR to revive the sick units. But there is tendency to declare the unit artificially sick and now BIFR has become a playground for unscrupulous business interest, in tandem with presiding officers in prolonging proceedings ad-infinitum, in subversion of the purpose with which these organizations were created. In all these, a fundamental flaw has been that there was no rigid time limit fixed for final decision.

A plethora of frauds is taking place in different industries. Advancement of technology and reach of the companies to global and rural market is putting Indian industries as well as department at higher risk of fraud. We face various fraud risks. Tentacles of the counterfeit market are spreading across the world. Boundaries are no barriers to those who fake it. For instance, in inventory management, fraud may arise while dealing with vendors. Collusion of vendors and employees can put a great loss to the company and the department. Apparently such employees would like to select a one time vendor instead of looking up for special and regular vendor in the system. So sometimes entire list of transaction has no identifying information for vendors.

In Telecom, there are many opportunities for frauds. There are huge number of subscribers, number of transaction or calls and the revenue throughout is huge. In Telecom Industry *'Psheudo - churn'* is a very common type of fraud. Defaulting individuals come back to the network with different names. Most frauds take place at the subscribers end. Due to advent of mobile device more contents move to mobile TV, contests, gaming etc. and it is very difficult to capture revenue. Technology driven products like credit cards are more susceptible to frauds. Data on the credit cards can be stolen, when a payment is made through a credit card, the card is away from sight for few minutes and it is taken by a low paid employee like waiter in restaurants etc. A data copying device smaller than pager can be clipped in a belt under the waiter's apron. When the card is swiped, data is copied on the device and within no time duplicate card is prepared. There is a plethora of data storing devices today which are leveraged by people with malicious intent. Confidential data may be stolen and copied on to several devices like pen drives, CD etc. and e-mailed to others. An investigator has to apply his mind and search for evidence.

The practice of pre-authentication of the invoices / gate passes has now been abolished and we always find computer generated invoice. Number of copies of similar invoice can be generated. One copy is sent while transporting the goods which can be destroyed at the destination if not checked in the route and again the same invoice may be used to accompany another goods. To check and prevent this there should be a checking *Naka* on the National Highways at specified distance similar to Toll Tax *Naka* where every goods transport vehicle would produce the accompanying documents which will be entered in the computer through photo device within no time. And then it will be automatically transferred to concerned department for cross tallying. Technology can help in detection of duplication of data. This system shall definitely check and prevent the movement of goods on parallel set of invoices and also availment of Cenvat credit on forged invoice.

The first battle against the fraud is won when the company's top management believes in good governance. Organization need to go beyond the traditional thoughts on corporate governance and lay out a complete risk management framework. Government will have to put robust mechanism, comprising of IT solution and processes to prevent fraud. There should be quick remedial action like punishment etc. so there is no recurrence. Fraud is a reputation risk, regulatory risk and a confidence risk. In a technologically advanced age a company needs to be more proactive towards preventing and combating frauds.

Domestic Indirect Taxes

The CII-Mckinsey report argues that total taxes on manufactured goods are 25 to 30 per cent of the retail price in India compared to 15 per cent in China and indirect tax contribute 50 per cent to the difference in retail prices between India and China. The Indian indirect tax structure is cost cascading and non-transparent and also imposes significant transaction-cum-cost compliance in business. Further the problem lies with complete waiver of indirect taxes on exported goods. It is reported that the CVD system does not work satisfactorily. Lower duties would have boosted the domestic market and permitted synergy between domestic and export markets.

In 2004-05 total tax revenue was 10.2 per cent of GDP from Central Taxes and further if State Tax is included the figure is more like 15 per cent. Given the Government expenditure this ratio should be 3 per cent more as share of GDP. As per Fiscal Responsibility and Budget Management Act (FRBM) the fiscal consolidation will occur via the revenue route rather than expenditure contraction route. Central tax revenue has stagnated at 10 per cent of GDP since 1990-1991. It was visualized an increase of 12.96 per cent in 2008-09 on the condition that tax reform takes place. The stagnation in indirect tax collection marks an increase in the direct tax collection from 1.9 per cent of GDP in 1990-91 to 4.5 per cent of GDP in 2004-05. The shares of Custom and Excise duties have declined. On the welfare side it is good that taxation through direct route is preferable to indirect taxation. However, in India this argument cannot be pushed too far. The share of direct and indirect taxes has been equally projected to 6.46 per cent in 2008-09. Thus, the share of indirect taxes should increase from present level. Indirect tax reform will work only if all the exemptions are withdrawn and rate of duty is reduced from present level. There should be a combined Goods and Service Tax (GST) with service sector taxation integrated into the NAT framework instead of tax on turnover. There should be unanimity on rate of VAT between Central and States.

Ways to reduce tax evasion

Tax evasion cannot be abolished but certainly it can be reduced to a great extent. No one wants to evade taxes and everyone desires to lead a respectful and peaceful life. Prestige has got greater value for everybody. Sometimes situations and circumstances lead them to adopt malpractices. How to reduce tax evasion is a burning question of the day. Readers must be aware of the first rule of administration namely "Broken Window Syndrome". According to this when a passer-by notices a window of a house broken and on his second visit again when it is not repaired or replaced, he gets the impression that there is no one to take care of the house. Next day another window of the house is also broken. An efficient and good management must immediately repair the broken window so that the message goes on. Similarly when a minor violation of rule is adequately and justifiably punished the message goes on and it forbids others from violation of rule.

There is a common excuse from tax evaders that it was their first instance of violation and have committed it due to ignorance of law but that is no excuse. If at the very first instance proper action under law is taken they would definitely feel and have an impression that evasion of tax is not easy and is punishable also. It is not good and can be severely punished if caught.

Sincerely by acting on the following, tax evasion can be reduced

1. Strengthening the tax administration.
2. Proper recognition for honest tax payers.

3. Honest tax payers should be suitably rewarded. Even in jail in USA tax payers are separately kept and receive better treatment.
4. Low rate of duty. It is a tested truth that lower rate of duty increases the total revenue collection.
5. Provision for incentive for voluntary tax compliance and payment.

Make IT a multi-pronged effort

The IT industry is set to touch $60 billion by 2010 from almost a scratch in the 1990s. The growth, over a two-decade span, is a fantastic achievement and a good example of what forward looking policy formulation can achieve. The industry can touch $500 billion over the next 10 years, even if it grows at a moderate rate of 20-25 per cent. While we celebrate the past success, it is to gauge how the industry can continue to grow at current rates over the next one to two decades, given the vast untapped market. This has to be seen in the context of the phase-out of the tax holiday enjoyed by companies in the software technology parks (STPI) in 2010. Merely focusing on extending this tax-break by a few more years would be short-sighted approach. The fact is, the industry is dominated by large companies - the top ten companies account for over 80 per cent of the total export. Larger IT companies are aggressively exploiting the special economic zone (SEZ) framework to lower their tax incidence. But restricting movement of business and resources between STPI and SEZ has introduced severe operational inefficiencies in these companies. Besides, revenues linked to intellectual property creation and products business is miniscule. Large companies also do very little outsourcing and contracting. Not just this. The IT industry puts tremendous pressure on urban infrastructure requirements and most of these companies do not participate in the development or partnering for infrastructure. The quality of human resources also continues to be a major concern. And growth is still centred around half a dozen big cities. Exports were crucial in the early 90s, but perhaps not any more.

Encourage SMES

We need to make policy changes now to correct some of the above anomalies and the first place to start is by encouraging SMEs. Today, companies of all sizes are treated the same way for tax purposes. Instead, let us create a differential tax structure and ensure that smaller companies continue to enjoy zero tax and larger companies pay tax. The Government has been resisting the demand to extend STPI benefit primarily to not let go of the huge tax revenues from the IT industry. The suggestion here is for Government to collect its targeted revenues from the larger companies and keep it zero tax for SMEs. Additionally, for all Government IT needs that are outsourced, insist on a certain percentage of work to be directly given to the SMEs by the Primary Vendor. We can also provide tax and other incentives to the larger IT companies for all outsourcing done to the SME companies to encourage sub-contracting within the industry. Sub-contracting and ancillary unit development is a big part of most industries and we should enable the same in the IT industry.

Differential treatment

The next big area for correction in policy is related to differential treatment of companies in STPI/SEZs though they are in the same business. We need to examine the idea of an SEZ for IT industry and the way it is implemented now. To begin with, most of the larger companies are using SEZs as a way purely to reduce taxes and it is debatable whether there is really new business coming which otherwise would not have come. The IT industry is also not capital-intensive (as can be seen from some of their zero debt balance sheets) and hence the benefits in importing equipment or technology are very limited. These companies need to grow in India and they would do so irrespective of SEZs. Majority of the IT SEZs are also continuing to get created in the existing IT corridors. Hence, SEZs for IT industry may not be serving their intended purpose. Therefore, the Government should decide on a certain tax rate it expects based on the size of the company and after that let the companies decide on where they would grow their business. This uniform taxation also takes away the mad rush for creation of SEZs in the country (a good percentage of which are predominantly coming for IT).

On a related plane, we should also discuss the need to bring domestic services on par with IT exports. The present framework encourages IT exports through various tax concessions. We incentivised exports in the 90s when the Balance of Payments (BOP) situation was precarious. Now, with the healthy forex reserves and the strengthening of the Rupee (barring the events when oil prices have changed some of this) preferential treatment for exports is no longer relevant. The IT Services players get higher revenues and margins in the overseas market and are already incentivised to work on exports and we do not need to further encourage this through tax concessions. The incentives for exports are working as disincentives to work in the domestic markets and we need to correct this by offering similar treatment to domestic services.

There are always concerns around how incentives for any specific targeted purpose may be misused. But today, there is a greater premium for companies to follow clean business practices and in any society an effectively implemented policy is the best recipe for success. We need to incentivise the industry to focus on the priority areas for the future and not shy away for fear of failure in implementation.

Drug companies who charge excise duty from consumers for price regulated medicines made in excise duty exempted states should pass on the excise benefit to consumers failing which it would amount to overcharging. The same is being taken care of by the National Pharmaceutical Pricing Authority (NPPA). Most of the large Indian and Multinational Companies have shifted their manufacturing plants to the excise duty exempted States as Himachal Pradesh, Uttarakhand, Jammu & Kashmir and Sikkim. There are 74 essential bulk drugs under direct price control. It appears the manufacturers are under the impression that excise benefit was being given not to pass any benefit to the customer but to attract investments in such states to develop their economy. The gain of excise duty was reduced by half when the Government reduced excise duty from 16 per cent to 8 per cent across sectors in the last budget. There are cases when drug companies misuse tax holiday benefit by labeling drug, made in excise free region as drugs made in excise levy States.

Fighting tax evasion calls for cooperation between Government and assessee. The Government must enact fair and effective policies to make it easy for tax payers to comply with their financial transaction like import and export. We need to be realistic. Developing countries often lack the resources to build effective tax system. By adopting the good practices in tax administration of other countries, accountability to democracy can be strengthened and corruption be combated effectively.

(b) CUSTOMS CASE

The year 1990-91, brought fundamental changes in our economic policies, taxation system and our way of thinking about these. But there has been a negative trend, which emerged due to our prevalent mind-set for sometimes which has not shown sign of slowing down. Their moral has not come up to the mark. They saw the shortcut to become rich in the liberalization of economy. There are abuses of export related incentives, specially the schemes like EPCG (Export Promotion Capital Goods), DEPB (Duty Exemption Pass Book), Replacement and other similar schemes.

I would like to discuss some of the cases of misuse of the schemes:

1. If someone was required to export quality garments, rags of low value were actually exported by him. Whereas he claimed export benefit of high value garments. Sometimes they import raw-material of high quality on the condition of use in the manufacture of final product meant for export, but they sell them in the market at premium price and export low value goods and produce export certificate. Many a time these substandard products are rejected by the buyers and there is no purchaser in the foreign country and they are thrown in the the sea as the cost of bringing the goods back in the country is more than the actual cost of the goods. They have already earned profit on their investment. The Law Enforcing Agencies fail to catch hold of such persons as they have already settled in Dubai.
2. Some of the scrupulous exporters chose to use the remote areas at the Indo-Nepal border where there is no proper road and communication system. They have claimed export incentives against export of goods through land customs worth hundreds of crores without actually exporting the goods.
3. I would also like to discuss one case of seizure of 1300 bars of gold by one of the famous officers of the customs department Sri Dayashankar, IRS. The said seized goods valued at Rs 13 crores at that time were seized at Porbandar coast during his stay in 1984-88, by the coast guard patrol ship 'Varun' from an Arab dhow in one of its first voyages.

Dawood Ibrahim, one of the dreaded smuggler has once said that he would like to work under him. (as reported in the *Illustrated Weekly*).

Combating terrorism by customs

The menace of terrorism has seriously affected our entire country. It has today an all India sweep, from Kashmir in north to Kerala in south and Mumbai in west to Manipur in east. Recent martyr of Delhi Police Inspector Shri Mohan Chand Sharma while battling with terrorists involved in recent series of blast in different parts of Capital has compelled us to think about united combating of terrorism and joining hands with police in completely eradication of terrorism from our country. A grim scenario is building up which calls for a comprehensive strategy. Religious fanatics, Naxalites and North-East insurgents have a significant nexus with external forces which enable them to get weapons, ammunition and explosives from neighbouring countries. I will restrict my discussion only to the role of customs in this regard. Now let us see how customs is equipped with.

The responsibility of Customs is bigger in this way that it faces at first entry point inside the country either at Airport or at Sea Port. If thorough checking of baggage at International Airport and scanning of containers is done at Sea Port there are every chances to restrict the entry of foreign made deadly weapons, chemical used in manufacturing of bombs which causes blast. Ammonium nitrate is said to be used in bombs. Now terrorists are also trying for hydrogen peroxide bombs. Given the wide usage of ammonium nitrate in fertilizers, NTHA taking a cue from laws governing explosives in US and UK, has proposed that only the higher arid more potent grades of compound may be banned, while leaving the inert grades for use in fertilizers. Though an inter ministerial panel has been looking at the possibilities of updating the Explosive Acts/Rules for a year now, the reservation of the Fertilizer Ministry against regulation of ammonium nitrate, a key ingredient in fertilizer is yet to be approved.

Empower with better infrastructure and remove restrictions, get the result. Paucity of funds is not a problem now. The cost of collection of indirect tax has gradually reduced from 0.84% to

0.57 per cent and 1 per cent of the revenue on exceeding the target of last fiscal is yet to be expensed. The present X-Ray machine at the Airports is mainly designed for the detection of narcotics and Pschvcotropic substances and metals of heavy specific gravity like gold and silver. The trained sniffer dogs have also been provided to Air Intelligence Unit at the Airport for the detection of narcotics. Looking to the present scenario the high quality X-Ray machine supported by a chemical laboratory well equipped with modern and latest testing equipments be provided at all the International Airports and Sea Ports for fast detection which would enhance the quality of work of the preventive wing of file customs.

In this connection Government has already made various Acts like WMD Act, 2005 which was enacted in June, 2005, and is an integrated and overriding legislation for WMD, delivery system related materials, equipment and technology. The Act supplements and compliments the existing Acts. It criminalize the range of unlawful accounts in relation to weapons of mass destruction and other means of delivery. After Iran-Iraq war in which chemicals were extensively used, Government has setup NACWC and empowered them with CWC Act (Chemical Weapons Convention) on the basis of discussion held in first Global Multilateral Disarmament Treaty. We have Atomic Energy Act, 1962. There is complete onus on the exporter to declare that it is not prohibited item. Uranium, Plutonium, Thorium, Beryllium and Deuterium are nuclear materials and prohibited for exports. Heavy water and Graphite are non-nuclear material. Import of dual used chemicals are allowed for peaceful purposes but denied for warfare. In response to 9/11 attack, clandestine proliferation and heightened fears of WMD UNSCR-1540 objective is to impose binding on non-proliferation of nuclear and biological weapons.

Section 135 of the Customs Act, 1962 has been duly amended to empower Custom Officer to seize and prosecute under various Acts discussed above. Board has also Issued circular No. 394/152/2002-cus (AS) dated 24.1.03 and cir no. 54/2005 cus. dated

30.12.05 in this regard. We have control on export also. Appendix 3 of schedule 2 of 11-C MS) of Foreign Trade Policy gives us the list of dual use chemicals. There was a SMET in 1995 which was renamed and amended to SCOMET 2000 and now further amended as SCOMET 2005 (special chemical organism material equipment technology). There are seven categories under which different items are categorized. Category O is for nuclear material which is completely banned for export. Application for export licence for SCOMET items are considered by DGFT and enduse certificate is given by the customs. The export application is placed before an inter ministerial working group and only after its approval license for export is issued.

We are nuclear power and we have to behave responsibily to sustain and enhance our prestige.

Compact Strike Force for Anti-Smuggling Operations

The compact teams formed on the basis of work ethos founded on four 'P's—precision, planning, pluck and presence of mind—is required to successfully face the current smuggling trend in the country. Intelligence must be honed to precision. Premature move may abort. The next is planning. One who has the intelligence can weigh all options and plan meticulously. Time is always with such team. On the spot things may not always go according to plan. One must always be mentally prepared for this. Courage and presence of mind are put to severe test at this stage. These two have to complement each other. Such teams, having all these can detect numerous cases of high values contrabands, investigate difficult cases and conduct risky operations of searches, surveillance, chase and arrests invariably with remarkable success. Small teams prompt each member to be on his toe and put every thing into the ongoing operations and thus more than make up for the numbers. These compact teams always proved one too many.

Anti-smuggling work is a logical extension of the basic functions of a custom officer which is to ensure that import and export goods pay duty and other taxes in accordance with law and further at the International airport their function is to facilitate tourists arriving in the country from abroad. Law not only means custom law which prescribes the rate of duties and procedures for importing and exporting of such goods but also other related laws such as Import and Export Policy which prescribes certain prohibitions and restrictions. If the basic law is violated in respect of any goods it amounts to smuggling. A simple example would be an attempt to land, say, a consignment of mobile phone of sea-coast. Goods can be imported only through a customs port on payment of duty. At the customs port, they are not only required to follow a set of procedures but also produce an import license. In case of missing of all these elements it would amount to smuggling.

The anti-smuggling work is perhaps a bit of aberration for a customs officer and since the basic function is collection of revenue only a fraction of its strength is deployed in anti-smuggling work. During the decades when smuggling was rampant, the limited resources of the customs were stretched to the limit. Numerical strength has never been a force of the customs and its limited numbers are concentrated in important ports and cities of the country, their presence sparse in the rest of the country. The DRI is a specialized intelligence and investigation wing of customs. Its zonal unit is all over in the major cities of the country. This organization is grueling regimen and calls for optimum utilization of the limited resources. This organization has evolved its own work ethos. Not every one opts for it. Those who do are the ones whom nothing can deflect or coerce or tempt away from the single minded pursuit of an idea or an objective. No risk is too grave for them and no reward greater.

Customs and Environment Protection

India has been playing a proactive role in the activities of the World Customs Organisation (WCO) in the international sphere. Several times, India has the distinction of being a WCO Policy Commission member and vice chair of the WCO Asia Pacific Region and currently is member of the Finance Committee of the WCO, India continues to play a major role in assisting the developing countries in capacity building. WCO has dedicated 2009 as International Customs Day to the cause of environment with the theme; Customs and the Environment : Protecting our Natural Heritage. This will give customs an ideal opportunity to highlight their role in protecting the environment since one of the crucial elements is to combat this crime at the International Borders.

India is one of the mega biodiversity centres in the world and has two of the world's 18 biodiversity hotspots located in the Eastern Himalays and in the Western Ghats. The sheer diversity of its terrestrial marine and other aquatic ecosystems ranging from the vast beaches of 7500 km of coastline, extensive forests, soaring mountains, sprawling deserts, wetlands and coral reefs is worth preserving. The country has fascinating presence of close to 49000 plant species and 81000 animal species accounting for 12.5 per cent for the world's flora and 6.6 per cent of its fauna.

As customs is engaged in prevention of illegal trafficking of 'goods' across borders, the 'goods' under the Customs Act covers wide range—antiques, object of art and literature, arms and ammunition, counterfeit currency, narcotics, drugs, ozone depleting substance (ODS), hazardous waste and material and endangered species of fauna and flora. Indian Customs in association with the WCO is further required to gear up their vigil at the border to guard theft of precious environment.

Import Duty

Import duties on raw material and intermediate goods should be reduced. Whereas the same should not be reduced in case of finished goods. Four tier import duty was recommended by Kelkar Task Force in 2000-07 ie 5 per cent for basic raw material, 8 per cent for intermediate goods, 10 per cent for finished goods other than consumer durables and 20 per cent for consumer durables. As per Doha Development Agenda started in 2001, Government is committed to reduce import duty. GATT/WTO system is not clear about reduction in import duty. There are plethora of Free

Trade Agreements (FTA) outside the WTO system involving manufactured product with zero duties. As long as there is resistance in general import duties the FTA problem will be there. So long as rule of origin and value addition is there, Customs formalities is bound to stay like EDI and online filing of declaration, self assessment of Bill of Entry, filing of IGM before arrival of cargo, deadlines for processing of documents payment of Custom duty through cheque and registration system of Custom House Agent. Further there are arguments that which Basic Custom duty may be zero, imported product may face Countervailing Duty (CVD) ie duty equivalent to domestic indirect taxes ie Central Excise Duty. That ignores State level Sales Tax and other taxes.

(c) INCOME TAX EVASION CASE

Recently, a trend has began by large companies improperly classifying employees as independent contractors. For example, one company has saved tax because it classified its drivers as independent contractors.

Below are just a few more examples of the ways people cheat on taxes:

- putting assets in another person's name
- failing to keep or concealing records of income
- paying by cash to avoid any written record of income
- claiming deductions that are bogus
- lying about ownership of assets
- mischaracterizing capital gains
- hiding assets overseas
- creating fictitious offshore companies
- embezzling funds or committing securities fraud (and not claiming it as income)

Global mergers & Income Tax Law

Overseas acquisitions not only comprise mega deals like acquisition of some foreign company but also include plenty of deals in the mid cap sectors fuelled by the fast growing ambitions of the Indian mid cap companies. However, one of the most peculiar trends which has been observed in almost all outbound deals is that Indian company tend to consolidate and integrate their investment and business structure of the companies acquired.

The Indian Income Tax Act provides for several tax concession to mergers/demergers of two Indian companies subject to the satisfaction of conditions laid down under section 2(1B) and Sec 2 (19AA) of the said Act, to be qualified as exempt mergers / demergers. Thus when a transfer of shares of a company, happens in an Indian mergers, there is a specific exemption under the Indian I-Tax Act on such transfer from capital gains tax. But the same is not applicable to foreign companies mergers i.e. when two foreign companies merge and the owner of foreign company is an Indian company. This issue should be judicially raised.

For example, when X Ltd. (US), a subsidiary of an Indian company get merged with another Y Ltd (US) a subsidiary of the same Indian company, then Y Ltd. would issue shares to Indian company the said transaction is taxable in India. The transaction is taxed in the hands of the shareholders, since there is a transfer of share held by him in the amalgamated company (i.e. X Ltd. US) in lieu of which he would be allotted shares in amalgamated company (i.e. Y Ltd. US). In the Indian mergers scenario the transaction would ideally be exempt in India on account of the specific exemption U/S 47 (vii). However, sec. 47 (vii) clearly states that this transaction would be tax exempt in the hands of the shareholders only if the amalgamated company is an Indian company.

Sec 47 (via) of the Indian I.T. Act, which specially exempts the tax on gains arising from transfer of share held by a foreign company, by way of amalgamation of foreign company with another foreign company, subject to satisfaction of certain conditions. However, the Act is silent as regards to a scenario where a foreign company, being a subsidiary of an Indian company, merges with another foreign company.

From the above, it can be concluded that in case of merger of foreign companies, the allotment of shares in the amalgamated foreign company in lieu of surrender of shares in amalgamated foreign company would be regarded as a transfer and hence would be chargeable to tax in India. Further, according to sec. 5(1) of the Indian I.T. Act, global income of an Indian company would also be covered in the scope of income of an Indian company. This being the case streamlining of the foreign shareholding of an Indian parent is taxed if the merging foreign company is a profitable company. This ideally brings a halt to all streamlining of foreign companies of India parent as it result in taxing gain which ordinarily stays within the group of companies has the structure of holding not been altered.

As there is no clarity on the taxation of foreign merger of companies held by the India parent the mechanism of computation of capital gains also does not exist. One possible way would be that proportionate net worth of the amalgamated company may be taken as the total sale consideration and from which cost of acquisition may be deducted.

Looking to the Indian company desire of global ambitions, it is imperative that the issue be addressed by the Income tax department specially. This will only facilitate quicker realization of synergies by Indian company from their overseas forays. One could also expect a pre-deal strutting if the streamlining tax neutral in the overseas jurisdiction.

Innovative ways of payment of direct taxes

After the terrorist attack in Mumbal on 26th Nov 08, one is intrigued by one placard which stood out in a peace procession. It read : NO MORE TAXES,WHY SHOULD WE PAY TAXES, IF WE CAN'T BE PROTECTED? Given this situation and emotions holding sway over Mumbaites, this outcry seemed justified. One can only hope that Mumbai and India may heal soon and concrete steps be taken to overcome this situations. In the US also tax payers are crying over the use of their money for bailouts. A unique suggestion has come out from US Congressman Louie Gohmert—a tax holiday for "we the people". If there is tax holiday, people could spend the amount in the markets and the economy would get much-needed relief. If taxes are not deducted from salary of January and Febuary, people could take and invest their own money where they believe it should go—paying down mortgages, buying a new car, making credit card payments. The economy would get relief where it is needed most. Even the self employed and small business owners would receive a fantastic amount of their own much needed money, and they will be able to invest and back into their businesses and even create the ability to hire more people.

One does not really know what happens to the education cess which one coughs up as part of tax dues? Please note that this is collected for a specific purpose—for educating India. Now, if instead of just paying this cess, if one deposits it at a school of one's choice wouldn't that be better? If we all know that the entire sum meant for the poor does reach him or her, wouldn't this direct payment system better? True, a handful of people may make fake payments. But patriotism burns strongly within each of us, at least in those who pay taxes and if it is for right cause most of them would pay willingly. Perhaps select schools could set up e-bank accounts, where deposits could be directly made. This would eliminate the middleman, reduce the cost of tax collection. Gurucharan Das, in one of his columns has written that India spends 14% of GDP in subsidies for the poor, which is more than enough to wipe out poverty. But poverty persists because subsidies leak out through corruption.

Even donations in kind like computer manufacturing company donating computer to government aided schools should be entitled to tax sops. While, this could be introduced, perhaps it is time to spread the net wider and make it possible for tax payers to give directly a portion of his tax for what it is meant for. And what better way to start than through education cess? In the words of Rabindranath Tagore: "Where the mind is led forward by thee into ever-widening thought and action into that heaven of freedom, my father let my country awake."

GST:

Shri Vijay Kelkar, Head of the Finance Commission and former Finance Secretary, after almost decades of effort estimates that the value of the GST (goods and service tax) reform to India will be $500 billion or almost half the GDP of India and therefore in his view it is the biggest reform in India since the delicensing reform in 1991. India is about to move to a unified GST to replace the current plethora of central and state in direct taxes. The Empowered Committee of State Finance Ministers is giving finishing touches to the GST which is due to be implemented by the year 2010-11. Canada is recognized as having a very good GST. According to professor Hamilton who is famous for computable general equilibrium model to estimate the impact to a well functioning GST on the economy came up with an estimated benefit of 1.4 per cent GDP for Canada. If we consider the similar level of benefit for India—an additional 1.4 per cent of GDP that is positive gain of $15 billion and after allowing the 3 per cent discount rate the present value of reform may be up to $500 billion. Moreover, the increased GDP may increase employment by 4-5 million. Further, it will restore rationally and ease of administration to an existing system already riddled with multiple authorities giving wage to corruption, evasion and distortion because of plethora of rates and exemptions levied by States and Centres. Cascading taxes badly hits the manufacturing in India when compared with taxes of other nations. Growth is also hold back by high rate of cascading taxes on capital goods.

Total income from Service Tax constitutes 55 per cent of GDP, while manufacturing contributes around 24 per cent of

GDP. Service Tax has plugged the tax gap to some extent. India needs a unified tax system coming from both services and manufacturing, taxing only the value addition at each stage. Presently exporters are unable to get full refunds of sundry indirect taxes, keeping them behind in global market competition. Shri Kelkar has indicated ways to improve the GDP after introduction of GST.

- GST will maximize coverage of goods and services and thus reduce the distortions and improve output.
- By introducing GST and ending over taxation it will make a huge long term difference to outcomes.
- A destination based GST will end the anomalies of the current system.
- GST will positively reduce the current systems red tape delay, hassels, corruption leakage and wastes.

But it is yet to be decided as to how the destination type regime of indirect taxes having no incidence on intermediate goods and services can come into being with the replacement of Central Excise and Central Sales Tax with Central GST and the replacement of all State level taxes with a State GST. The domestic producers, traders and exporters to whom tradable goods and services are delivered in the respective supply chains may not, in the absence of appropriate quantity shifts envisaged by the policy reforms, be able to claim credit for the prior-stage tax paid to the Union out of the liability to pay tax to a State at the next stage in the supply chain and vice-versa. The clear cut policy is required to be decided regarding issues relating to equitable distribution primarily by means of a direct tax-cum-direct subsidy regime, non-levy and partial and total exemptions.

CHAPTER 3 MONEY LAUNDERING

Money laundering is the practice of engaging in financial transactions in order to conceal the identity, source, and/or destination of money, and is a main operation of the underground economy. Money derived from certain criminal activity is legalised in money laundering. It is proceeds of crime, it takes place within the banking system. Money laundering provides legitimate cover to criminals. It also provides source of funds to crime. It may reduce the inflow of legitimate money in the domestic market. There is great risk to National Financial Institution. Through money laundering power accumulates in the hands of criminals.

In the past, the term "money laundering" was applied only to financial transactions related to organized crime. Today its definition is often expanded by government regulators (such as the United States Office of the Comptroller of the Currency) to encompass any financial transaction which generates an asset or a value as the result of an illegal act, which may involve actions such as tax evasion or false accounting. As a result, the illegal activity of money laundering is now recognized as potentially practised by individuals, small and large businesses, corrupt officials, members of organized crime (such as drug dealers or the Mafia), and even corrupt states, through a complex network of shell companies and trusts based in offshore tax havens. A few examples of money laundering are surfing or kiting.

The increasing complexity of financial crime, the increa recognized value of so-called "financial intelligence" (FININT combating transnational crime and terrorism, and the specul impact of capital extracted from the legitimate economy has to an increased prominence of money laundering in politic economic, and legal debate.

It is estimated that the size of money laundering worldwi through the banking sector, is more than US$ 500 billion to on trillion annually. A recent estimate has projected that worldwid money-laundering not only economically destabilizes a country but also exposes it to terrorist attacks, threatening its integrity and sovereignty. It conceals the huge, illegal profits generated by unscrupulous, organized criminal groups in various fields of crime. The culture of these groups is "criminogenic" and are "regulatory resistant". The speed and case of modern electronic finance have contributed a lot to the growth of this crime. Given the staggering volume of this crime, broad international cooperation between law enforcement and regulatory agencies is essential in order to identify the source of illegal proceeds, trace the fund to specific criminal activities and confiscate criminal's financial assets.

Money laundering involves bankers, lawyers, car dealers, real estates builders, accountants and also others, who allow their businesses to be used by someone to launder the proceeds of a crime.

Every country has its criminal underworld. The biggest organizations and the ones that have been active and have long standings can be found in the hubs of capitalism: the United States (Cosa Nostra), Europe (the Sicilian Mafia) and Asia (the Chinese Lriads and Japanese Yakusas).

What is Money Laundering?

The term money-laundering brings to our mind those nefarious activities of the criminals who provide an envelope to "slush funds" in order to exhibit those as genuine money. In other words, money-laundering is a process by which criminals give the colour of legality and legitimacy to slush funds. Ignoring economic vandalism, most of the crime is economic crime. In Black's Law of Lexicon the term laundering is being referred to as investment or other transfer of money flowing from racketeering, drug transactions and other sources (illegal sources) into legitimate channels so that its original source cannot be traced. Apart from the traditional activities of drugs, racketeering, kidnapping, gambling, procuring women and children, smuggling (alcohol, tobacco, medicines), armed robbery, counterfeiting and bogus invoicing, tax evasion and misappropriation of public funds, new markets are also flowering. These include smuggling, illegal labour and refugees, computer piracy, trafficking in works of art and antiquities, in stolen cars and parks, in protected species and human organs, forgery in arms, toxic and nuclear products, etc.

Money laundering generally involves a series of multiple transactions used to disguise the source of financial assets so that these assets may be used without compromising the criminals who are seeking to use the funds. These transactions fall into three stages i.e. Placement (Dirty money being inserted into the financial system through a process of deposits wire, transfers, or other means, unlawful proceeds into financial institutions.) Layering (Separates; the proceeds, room their criminal origin by moving them through a series of financial transactions. This makes it harder to establish a connection between them); and Integration (Creating a legitimate explanation for the source of funds, allowing them to be retained, invested or used to acquire goods or assets).

The characteristics of organized crime are quite evident in money laundering as it is a group activity which is long-term and continuing; a criminal activity which is carried out often by more than one person; an activity which is carried out irrespective of national boundaries at large scale; and generates proceeds, which are often made available for illicit use. Criminals involved in money laundering commit three basic types of crimes i.e. Crimes of passion or honour; Crimes of violence or vandalism; and Economic crimes — crime committed to make money. Most often crimes are committed for two reasons; for kicks (to prove that they can get away with it and for unscrupulous greed for quick money (they think that they can make more money from the crime than they can from the same amount of legitimate endeavours).

How it is done?

Some current estimates are that of US$ 500 billion to US$ 1 trillion in criminal proceeds are laundered through banks worldwide each year with about half of what is circulated through US banks [US Senate, Nov. 1999 & Feb. 2001]. As the banks are widely used for money laundering they have a central role to play in curbing the menace. Accordingly, the money laundering activities have been subject of eight prior investigations in U.S. According to the Permanent Subcommittee's Report, there are five major factors which create money laundering vulnerabilities: the role of private bankers, private banks as client advocates, powerful customers, and a corporate culture of secrecy, a corporate culture of lax controls and the competitive nature of the industry.

Private Bankers as Client Advocates

Private bankers are the linchpin of the private bank system. They are trained to service their clients and to set up accounts and move money around the world using sophisticated financial systems and secrecy tools. Private banks encourage their bankers to develop personal relationships with their clients, visiting the client's homes, attending weddings and graduations, and arranging their financial affairs. The result is that private bankers may feel loyalty to their clients for both professional and personal reasons, leading them to miss or minimize warning signs. In addition, private bankers use their expertise in bank systems to evade what they may perceive as unnecessary "red tape" hampering the services their clients want, thereby evading controls designed to detect or prevent money laundering.

Powerful Clients

Private bank clients are, by definition, wealthy. Many also exert political or economic influence which may make banks anxious to satisfy their requests and reluctant to ask hard questions. If a client is a government official with influence over the bank's in-country operations, the bank has added reason to avoid offence. Moreover verifying information about a foreign client's assets, business dealings, and community standing can be difficult for US banks. The Federal Reserve board found in its private banking review that foreign clients were particularly difficult for private banks to assess due to a lack of independent data bases of information, suit as credit reports. While private banks routinely claim that their private bankers gain intimate knowledge of their clients, the case histories demonstrate that too often is not true. For example, in one case, a private banker was unaware for more than three years that he was handling the accounts of one of the African heads of state.

Culture of Secrecy

A culture of secrecy pervades the private banking industry. Numbered accounts at Swiss banks are but one example. There are other layers of secrecy that private banks and clients routinely use to mask accounts and transactions. For example, private banks routinely create shell companies and trusts to shield the identify of the beneficial owner of a bank account. Private banks also open accounts under code names and will, when asked, refer to clients by code names of encode account transactions.

Secrecy Jurisdictions

In additions to shell corporations and codes, a number of private banks also conduct business in secrecy jurisdictions such as Switzerland and Cayman Islands, which impose criminal sanctions on the disclosure of bank information, related to clients and restrict US bank oversight. The secrecy laws are so light, they even restrict internal bank oversight.

Culture of Lax Controls

In addition to secrecy, private banking operates in a corporate culture that is at times indifferent or resistant to anti-money laundering controls, such as due diligence requirements and accounts monitoring. The problem begins with the private banker, who, in most private banks, is responsible for the initial enforcement of anti-money laundering controls. It is the private banker who is charged with researching the background of prospective clients, and it is the private banker who is asked in the first instance to monitor existing accounts for suspicious activity. But it is also the job of the private banker to open accounts and expand client deposits. According to John Reed, Co-chairman of Citigroup (with 30 years of banking experience), private bankers tend to become advocates for their clients and has lost the detachment needed to monitor their transactions. He also observed that private bankers often don't have the temperament or discipline needed to ask clients detailed questions about their funds and transactions and to record the information provided in a proper form.

The fundamental problem is that private bankers are being asked to fill contradictory roles to develop a personal relationship with a client and increase their deposits with the bank, while also monitoring their accounts for suspicious activity and questioning specific transactions. Human nature makes these contradictory roles difficult to perform, and anti-money laundering duties often suffer.

Private Banks have dealt with this problem by setting up systems to ensure that private banker activities are reviewed by third parties, such as supervisors, compliance personnel or auditors. The subcommittee staff investigation has found, however, that while strong oversight procedures exist on paper, in practice private bank oversight is often absent, weak or ignored.

Cut throat Competition

Another factor creating money laundering concern is the ongoing competition among private banks for clients, due to profitability of the business. A Federal Report on private banking states. : "As the target market for private banking is growing, so is the level of competition among institutions that provide private banking services" [FRB, 1997]. Private Banks interviewed by the subcommittee staff confirm that the markets remain highly competitive; some also reported to have plans to expand operations. The dual pressures of competition and expansion are disincentives for private banks to impose tough anti-money laundering controls that may discourage new business or cause existing clients to move to other institutions.

In addition to the general factors cited above, the actual products and services offered by the private bank also create opportunities for money laundering.

1. **Multiple Accounts:** A striking feature of the private bank accounts examined is their complexity. Private bank clients often have many accounts in many locations. Some are personal checking, money market or credit card accounts. Others are in the name of one or more shell companies and multiple investment accounts are common, including mutual funds, stock, bonds and time deposits. The reality right now is that private banks allow clients to have multiple accounts in multiple locations under multiple names and do not aggregate the information. This approach creates vulnerabilities to money laundering by making it difficult for banks to have a comprehensive understanding of their own client's accounts. In addition, it complicates regulatory oversight and law enforcement, by making it difficult for banks to have a comprehensive understanding of their own clients' accounts. It also complicates regulatory oversight and law enforcement, by making it nearly impossible for an outside reviewer to be sure that all private bank accounts belonging to an individual have been identified.

2. **Secrecy Products:** Most private banks offer a number of products and services that shield a client's ownership

of funds. They include offshore trusts and shell corporations, special name accounts, and codes used to refer to clients or fund transfers.

3. **Movements of Funds:** Current account transactions at private banks routinely involve large sums of money. The size of client transaction increases the banks vulnerability to money laundering by providing an attractive venue for money launderers who want to move large sums without attracting notice. In addition, most private banks provide products and services that facilitate the quick, confidential and hard-to-trace movement of money across jurisdictional lines.

4. **Credit:** Another common private bank service involves the extension of credit to clients. Several private bankers told the subcommittee that private banks urge their private bankers to convince clients to leave their deposits in the bank and use them as collateral for large loans. This practice enables a bank to earn a fee not only on the deposits under their management, but also on the loans. This practice also however, creates vulnerability for money laundering by allowing a client to deposit questionable funds and replace them with "clean" money from a loan. Moreover, as the client loans are fully collaborative by assets on deposits with the bank, the bank may not scrutinize the loan purpose and repayment prospects as carefully as for a conventional loan, and may unwittingly further a money launderer's efforts to hide illicit proceeds behind seemingly legitimate transactions.

5. **Development of Off-Shore Banking:** Originally, off-shore centers were quite literally islands, hence the expression. Today the term is used rather loosely for financial centers, which operate within a low tax regime; this enables international transfers of money to take place

with a great deal of facility and with no hindrance to capital flows.

i. The development of the offshore banking sector has made it difficult to prevent money laundering.

ii. As Helmut Schmidt once observed, central banks "did not see that they were losing their grip over the markets when they allowed commercial banks to establish offshore affiliations."

iii. Governments regard it as synonymous with enhanced competitiveness.

iv. Competitiveness is deemed to be inconsistent with tight monitoring and control, and offshore banks and corporations attract funds largely because they promise both anonymity and the possibility of tax avoidance, and in some cases, tax evasion.

v. The Cayman Islands, the Netherlands Antilles, Aruba and Cyprus are all examples of offshore banking havens that have been used or confirmed to be used by criminal organizations for laundering the proceeds from their illicit activities.

vi. Such centers offer offshore attractive opportunities for the transfer and secretion of funds in places where they are relatively safe from identification and seizure by law enforcement.

vii. Most often, offshore corporations are created simply to launder and hide money.

World's Worst Banking Scandal: The world's worst banking scandal, inflicting huge financial losses on thousands of people worldwide, surfaced in the media in 1991. This was the Bank of Credit and Commerce International (BCCI). As could be expected, it had heavy ties with the CIA, terrorist organizations, drug traffickers, and any other crooked financial transactions shunned by most other banks. It financed terrorist activities, financial drug trafficking deals, defrauded depositors. Years before it was shut down, Robert Gates, FBIO Chief, referred to BCCI as the Bank of Crooks and Criminals.

BCCI started operations in Pakistan in 1972, with much of its funding provided by Bank of America and the CIA. Bank of America claims that it sold its BCCI interest in the early 1980s, but records show that Bank of America continued to control much of BCCI's operations until shortly before BCCI was shut down. In the early 1970s, CIA operative Gunther Russbacher transferred sizable amounts of CIA funds into the bank for the start-up operations.

The CIA knew about BCCI's activities, and found its mindset to be very manipulating and planned its own operations through BCCI. BCCI was customers made for the covert and corrupt activities of the CIA, the MOSSAD, drug dealers and terrorists. CIA operatives used the bank to launder money from CIA enterprises, including drug trafficking proceeds, and from its various financial activities within the United States, including its use of savings and loans, to fund unlawful arms shipments, finance terrorist operations, undermine foreign governments, and other covert activities. Investigating reports showed that BCCI was able to simultaneously manipulate the spy agencies of numerous countries, including the US, Israel, Pakistan, China, Saudi Arabia, among others. BCCI was supplying funds for terrorist organizations such as Abu Nidal. BCCI rigged international commodity markets that permitted certain insiders to make hundreds of million of dollars in profits, offset by the same amount lost by depositors. BCCI was laundering money (drug money) for drug cartels throughout the world.

Frauds from Small Bank Accounts

The "fraudsters" use fake certificates of deposit drawn on other branches of an international bank, which can range from US$10 million to US$ 25 million. The "fraudsters" also use fund transfers, which involve real dollars, opening up small accounts into which they then pour millions of dollars. "Fraudsters" will also use counterfeit letters of agreement, drawn on bank letter-heads, seemingly vouching for a client from another branch of that bank, or confirming a deal has been approved etc. The problem which creates a temptation to approve such transactions is that these banks may be turning away legitimate business. Thus there is concern that banks operating overseas may be at a competitive disadvantage because they adhere to standards for "knowing your customers" identifying beneficial owners of transactions refusing suspicious or unusual transactions, etc. The banks should be advised informally that the answer is not to lower standards in the home country or abroad, but to intensify efforts to ensure that all major financial centers operate within the limits of an international consensus on counter measures.

What Bankers need to know: Anti-Money Laundering Controls?

International banking continues to grow, developing worldwide connections among banks, as well as the increasing sophistication of banking methods. The constant challenge is to ensure that every bank can account for its customers. Every government has laws which ensure the prosecution of financial crimes, and that every society sets moral and ethical standards for the conduct of commerce. Many important financial centers have now adopted legislation to curb drug related money laundering, and the number of governments which have ratified the 1988 UN Convention continued to increase. But the race between criminals seeking new ventures, and oversight bodies seeking more widespread compliance, still goes to the crooks.

The act of "money laundering" was not invented during the Prohibition era in the United States, but many techniques were developed and refined then. Many methods were devised to disguise the origins of money generated by the sale of illegal alcoholic beverages. Following Al Capone's 1931 conviction for tax evasion, mobster Meyer Lansky transferred funds from Florida "carpet joints" (small casinos) to accounts overseas. After the 1934 Swiss Banking Act, which created the principle of bank secrecy, Meyer Lansky bought a Swiss bank to which he would transfer his illegal funds through a complex system of shell companies, holding companies, and offshore accounts.

The term "money laundering" does not derive, as is often said, from Al Capone having used laundromats to hide ill-gotten gains. It was Meyer Lansky who perfected money laundering's older brother, "capital flight," transferring his funds to Switzerland and other offshore places. The first reference to the term "money laundering" itself actually appears during the Watergate scandal. US President Richard Nixon's "Committee to Reelect the President" moved illegal campaign contributions to Mexico, then brought the money back through a company in Miami. It was Britain's *Guardian* newspaper that coined the term, referring to the process as "laundering."

This is usually used when there is cocaine or some other kind of substance related to drug.

Examples

If a person is making thousands of dollars in small change a week from a business (not unusual for a store owner) and wishes to deposit that money in a bank, it cannot be done without possibly drawing suspicion. In the United States, for example, cash transactions and deposits of more than a certain dollar amount are required to be reported as "significant cash transactions" to the Financial Crimes Enforcement Network (FinCEN), along with any other suspicious financial activity which is identified as "suspicious activity reports." In other jurisdictions suspicion-based requirements are placed on financial services employees and firms to report suspicious activity to the authorities. Methods to conceal the source are therefore required.

Irregular funding

One method of keeping this small change private would be for an individual to give money to an intermediary who is already legitimately taking in large amounts of cash. The intermediary would then deposit that money into an account, take a premium, and write a cheque to the individual. Thus, the individual draws no attention to himself, and can deposit his cheque into a bank account without drawing suspicion. This works well for *one-off* transactions, but if it occurs on a regular basis then the cheque deposits themselves will form a paper trail and could raise suspicion.

Captive business

Another method involves establishing a business whose cash inflow cannot be monitored, and funneling the small change into this business and paying taxes on it. All bank employees however are trained to be constantly on the lookout for any transactions which appear to be an attempt to get around the currency reporting requirements. Such shell companies should deal directly with the public, perform some service-related activity as opposed to providing physical goods, and reasonably accept cash as a matter of business. Dealing directly with the public ensures plausible anonymity of source.

An example of a legitimate business displaying plausible anonymity of source would be a hairstylist. Since it would be unreasonable for them to keep track of the identity of their customers, a record of their transaction amounts must be ostensibly accepted as *prima facie* evidence of actual financial activity. Service-related businesses have the advantage of anonymity of resources. A business that sells computers has to account for where it actually got the computers, whereas a plumbing company merely has to account for labour, which can be falsified. Reasonably accepting cash means the business must regularly perform services that total less than $500 on average, since above that amount most people pay with a check, credit card, or other traceable payment method. The company should actually function on a legitimate level. In the plumbing company example, it is perfectly reasonable for a lot of the business to involve only labour (no parts), and for some business to be paid for in cash, but it is unreasonable for all of their business to involve no parts and only cash payment. Therefore the legitimate business will generate a legitimate level of parts usage, as well as enough traceable transactions to mask the illegitimate ones.

Corrupt politicians and lobbyists also launder money by setting up personal non-profits to move money between trusted organizations, so that donations from inappropriate sources may be illegally used for personal gain.

Legal considerations

Many jurisdictions adopt a list of specific predicate crimes for money laundering prosecutions as a "self launderer" (the UK has an "all-crimes" regime). In addition, AML/CFT laws typically have other offences such as "tipping off," "willful blindness," not reporting suspicious activity, and conscious facilitation of a money launderer/terrorist financier to move his/her monies.

UK legislation

The "money laundering" legislation in the United Kingdom, under Sections 327 to 340 of the Proceeds of Crime Act 2002 (PoCA), and all of the Money Laundering Regulations 2003 and 2007, is wide-ranging and encompasses mere possession of criminal or terrorist property as well as its acquisition, transfer, removal, use, conversion, concealment, or disguise. In the UK "money laundering" need not involve money (it relates to assets of any kind, both tangible and intangible, and to the avoidance of a liability) and need not involve laundering either (a thief's possession of the assets he himself stole is included). There is no lower limit to what has to be reported — a suspicious transaction involving a single £5 note may be required to be reported. All persons (not just financial services employees and firms) are technically required to report, and obtain consent for their own involvement in crime or suspicious activities involving money or assets of any kind. So in the UK a thief who steals a vest from a clothes store commits a "money laundering" offence because he has possession of an asset derived from crime. He is technically required to seek consent from law enforcement for his continued possession of the vest if he is to avoid risk of prosecution for "money laundering."

The UK legislation also creates a money laundering offence where a person enters into, or becomes concerned in, an arrangement which facilitates (by whatever means) the acquisition, retention, use, or control of criminal property by another person. This has impacted upon lawyers and other professional advisers in the UK who act for a client whom they suspect may possess criminal property of any kind.

Because the UK legislation is wide-ranging, the UK FIU authority, the Serious Organised Crime Agency, receives a large volume of suspicious activity reports (SARs) - in 2005 just under 200,000 SARs were received. The number of SARs received appears to be growing by almost 50% each year.

The UK legislation was relaxed slightly in 2005 to allow banks and financial institutions to proceed with low value transactions involving suspected criminal property without requiring specific consent for every transaction (but the reporting of all transactions is still required).

American legislation

The Bank Secrecy Act of 1970 requires banks to report cash transactions of $10,000.01 or more. The Money Laundering Control Act of 1986 further defined money laundering as a federal crime. The USA PATRIOT Act of 2001 expanded the scope of prior laws to more types of financial institutions, added a focus on terrorist financing, and specified that financial institutions take specific actions to "know your customer" (KYC).

In the United States, Federal law provides (in part): "Whoever ... knowingly ... conducts or attempts to conduct ... a financial transaction which in fact involves the proceeds of specified unlawful activity ... with the intent to promote the carrying on of specified unlawful activity ... shall be sentenced to a fine of not more than $500,000 or twice the value of the property involved in the transaction, whichever is greater, or imprisonment for not more than twenty years, or both."

While money laundering typically involves the flow of "dirty money" (criminal proceeds) into a "clean" bank account or negotiable instrument, terrorist financing frequently involves the reverse flow: apparently clean funds converted to "dirty" purposes. A hawala may launder drug proceeds and help fund a terrorist, netting the incoming and outgoing funds with only occasional small net settlement transactions.

Jurisprudence

The Supreme Court of the United States on June 2, 2008, rendered 2 judgments in favour of defendants, narrowing the application of the federal money-laundering statute. First, in a 9-0 decision, ponente Justice Clarence Thomas reversed Acuna, Mexico's Humberto Cuellar's conviction and ruled that "hiding $81,000 in cash under the floorboard of a car and driving toward Mexico is not enough to prove the driver was guilty of money laundering; instead, prosecutors must also prove the driver was traveling to Mexico for the purpose of hiding the true source of the funds." The Court further ruled "that federal prosecutors have gone too far in their use of money laundering charges to combat drug traffickers and organized crime; that money laundering charges under the Money Laundering Control Act of 1986, Sec. 18 U. S. C. § 1956(a)(2)(B)(i) apply only to profits of an illegal gambling ring and cannot be used when the only evidence of a possible crime is when a courier headed to Texas-Mexico border with $ 81,000 in cash (proceeds of a marijuana transaction); it cannot be proven merely by showing that the funds were concealed in a secret compartment of a Volkswagen Beetlecar; instead, prosecutors must show that the purpose of transporting funds in a money laundering case was to conceal their ownership, source or control; the secrecy must be part of a larger "design" to disguise the source or nature of the money." Second, in a 5 to 4 ruling, Justice Antonin Scalia reversed Efrain Santos of Indiana and Benedicto Diaz's convictions for money laundering based on cash from an illegal lottery. Scalia ruled that the law referred to the "proceeds of some form of unlawful activity; paying off gambling winners and compensating employees who collect the bets don't qualify as money laundering; the word "proceeds" in the federal money-laundering statute, 18 U.S.C. §1956, and §1956(a)(1)(A)(i) and§1956(h), applies only to transactions involving criminal profits, not criminal receipts; those are expenses, and prosecutors must show that profits were used to promote the illegal activity." Congress enacted the 1986 statute after the President's Commission on Organized Crime stressed the problem of "washing" criminal proceeds through overseas bank accounts and legitimate businesses. It imposes a 20-year maximum prison term and heavy fines.

Legislation in India

In India Prevention of Money-Laundering Act, 2002 has been passed which came into effect since 1st of July, 2005. As per Section 3 of the Act, offence of money-laundering covers those persons or entities who directly or indirectly attempts to indulge or knowingly assists or knowingly is a party or is actually involved in any process or activity connected with the proceeds of crime and projecting it as untainted property, such person or entity shall be guilty of offence of money-laundering.

Section 4 of the Act prescribes punishment for money-laundering with rigorous imprisonment for a term which shall not be less than three years but which may extend to seven years and shall also be liable to fine which may extend to five lakh rupees and for the offences mentioned in paragraph 2 of Part A of the Schedule, the punishment shall be upto ten years.

Section 12 (1) prescribes the obligation on Banking companies, financial institutions and intermediaries (a) to maintain certain records detailing the nature and value of the transaction which may be prescribed, whether such transactions comprise of a single transaction or a series of transactions integrally connected to each other, and where such series of transactions take place within a month; 12 (b) to furnish information of transactions referred to in clause (a) to the Director within such time as may be prescribed and to (c) verify and maintain the records of the identity of all its clients. As per Section 12 (2), the records referred to in sub-section (1) as mentioned above, is required to be maintained for a period of ten years from the date of cessation of the transactions between the clients and the banking company or financial institution or intermediary, as the case may be.

The provisions of the Act is frequently reviewed and various amendments have been passed from time to time.

Bangladesh legislation

In Bangladesh, the issue of money laundering has been dealt with by the Prevention of Money Laundering Act, 2002 (Act No. VII of 2002). In terms of section 2 of the Prevention of Money Laundering Act, 2002 , "Money Laundering means (a) Properties acquired or earned directly or indirectly through illegal means; (b) Illegal transfer, conversion, concealment of location or assistance in the above act of the properties acquired or earned directly of indirectly through legal or illegal means." In this Act, "Properties means movable or immovable properties of any nature and description".

Fighting money laundering

The primary method of anti-money laundering is the requirement on financial intermediaries to know their customers — usually termed KYC (know your customer) requirements. With good knowledge of their customers, financial intermediaries will often be able to identify unusual or suspicious behaviour, including false identities, unusual transactions, changing behaviour, or other indicators that laundering may be occurring. But for institutions with millions of customers and thousands of customer-contact employees, traditional ways of knowing their customers must be supplemented by technology. Bank and corporate security directors can also play an important role in fighting money laundering.

Using information technology

Information technology can never be a replacement for a well-trained investigator, but as money laundering techniques become more sophisticated, so too is the technology used to fight it. Before anti-money laundering programs became commonplace, the Bank Secrecy Act required financial institutions to file Currency Transaction Reports (CTR) for cash transactions of $10,000 or more in the U.S. These CTRs prove invaluable for investigators, but money launderers began to structure their transactions to avoid the reporting requirements. As a result, the U.S. passed laws against structuring transactions to avoid the reporting requirements, and most structuring would trigger a Suspicious Activity Report by the financial institution.

Current anti-money laundering software packages include capabilities of name analysis, rules-based systems, statistical and profiling engines, neural networks, link analysis, peer group analysis, and time sequence matching. In addition, there are specific KYC solutions that offer case-based account documentation acceptance and rectification, as well as automatic risk scoring of the customer (taking account of country, business, entity, product, transaction risks) that can be reviewed intelligently. Other elements of AML technology include portals to share knowledge and e-learning for training and awareness.

Financial Crimes Enforcement Network (FinCEN), is an organization created by the United States Department of the Treasury. FinCEN receives Suspicious Activity Reports from financial institutions, analyses them, and shares their data with U.S. law enforcement agencies and equivalent Financial Intelligence Units (FIUs) of other countries. One of its strategic goals is to improve information-sharing through Government. It offers training and advice to organizations of foreign governments to help improve the efficacy of their anti-money laundering programs..

September 11, 2001 and the international response to the underground economy

After September 11, 2001, money laundering became a major concern of the United States' *war on terror*, although critics argue that it has become less and less an important matter for the White House. Based in Luxembourg, Clearstream International, a central securities depository and clearing house or "bank of banks" which practices "financial clearing," centralizing debit, and credit operations for hundreds of banks, was accused of being a major operator of the underground economy via a system of un-published accounts; Bahrain International Bank, owned by Osama bin Laden, would have profited from these transfer facilities. The scandal prompted Andre Lussi, Clearstream's CEO, to resign on December 31, 2001; several judicial investigations were opened; and the European Commission was interpelled by Members of the European Parliament (MEPs) Harlem Desir, Glyn Ford, and Francis Wurtz, who asked the Commission to investigate the accusations and to ensure that the June 10, 1990 directive (91/308 CE) on control of financial establishment was applied in all member states, including Luxembourg, in an effective way.

The international response to the underground economy has been coordinated by the Financial Action Task Force on Money Laundering ("FATF," also known by its French acronym of "GAFI"), whose original 40 principles form the basis of most international responses to money laundering activity. A further 8 principles, designed to counteract funding to terrorist organisations, were added on June 30, 2003, in response to the September 11, 2001, with another added 22 October 2004, to form what are now known as the "40 + 9" principles of anti-money laundering and combatting the financing of terrorism (AML/CFT). Compliance with, or a movement towards compliance with, these principles is now seen as a requirement of an internationally active bank or other financial service entity.

Amounts

Numerous regulatory and governmental authorities quote figures for estimated amounts of money laundered annually, either worldwide or within a national economy. A frequently cited figure is 2-5% of the worldwide global economy put forward by the IMF. However, it has been noted in academic circles that such figures are usually simply "best guesses". In 1997 the FATF, an arm of the OECD set up to combat money laundering, frankly admitted "the vast majority of FATF members lack sufficient data to support any credible estimate." Although admissions of that nature are no longer maintained, there is still a dearth of hard data as to the actual amounts of money laundered worldwide. Some academic commentators have expressed real concerns about the reliability and basis of figures used by governmental and multinational organizations.

> "We are faced with the problem that there has been little work to develop an objective academic analysis of the true extent of laundering, which means that we do not have a framework within which the appropriateness of legislative measures can be evaluated. Without this, it is difficult to challenge the 'alarmist' position of the authorities whereby such estimates have been put forward, quoted and repeated, becoming, through such repetition, seemingly established truths. It can be argued ... that global estimates are little more than informed guesses: "large numbers are frequently thrown around without serious support" (Reuter and Trumen, 2005, p.56), re-produced to the point at which they gain, through mere repetition, [they are perceived to have] some form of reliable accuracy."

Money laundering is the biggest fear for Finance Industry. The entire industry in the world or any separate country must understand that financial crime needs to be understood, analyzed and fought proactively. Banking industry needs to be one step ahead of money launderers in order to control the menace of money laundering and financial crimes. Concern regarding financial crime is growing to unprecedented levels amongst UK financial institutions, [Logic CMG Report, 2003] One of the best control techniques for the banks to control money laundering is to know your customer. [FSA Report, 2003]. The consultation paper, published in August 2003, describes the FSA's money laundering directions on two important anti-money laundering controls: One, issues relating to obtaining and using customer information for anti-money laundering purposes, and secondly on Anti- money laundering monitoring, assessing customers use firms' products and services and how possible money laundering activities can be identified from this.

Eleven world money centre banks agreed in October 2000 to a set of anti-money laundering guidelines for private banking activities. These guidelines state at the outset that "bank policy will be to prevent the use of its worldwide operations for criminal purposes."

SWIFT is the principal international service for wire transfer message trafficking that can initiate funds transfer. In Russia and some East European states, banks can be readily purchased for very little money — though few of them have electronic banking access to SWIFT. SWIFT is a co-operative society located in Belgium having 2600 institutions in 65 countries. It provides services to security bankers and dealers; clearing institutions; and recognized security exchanges.

This is what the future nightmare envisioned by the authorities will be like — with organized crime in control of banks and able to launder huge sums of money not only for themselves but also for other criminal organizations. Already in Russia it is said that criminal groups control over 400 banks and 47 exchanges. This is worrying bank chairmen in Russia as between 1994 and July

1995, there were thirty assassination attempts against top bank officials, sixteen of them were killed. These killings along with earlier ones were important indicators of the efforts by criminal organizations to infiltrate the Russian banking system. Infiltration of the banking system offers significant advantages for criminal organizations, not least the opportunity it gives to facilitate money laundering for both Russian and foreign criminal organizations. Russian officials have worked with FATF and US government agencies to put into place more effective regulations and proceedings to combat money laundering, in accordance with international standards.

In February 1988, the OECD's Financial Action Task Force for money laundering in its Annual Report highlighted the problem in Mexico and stated "One of the most favoured technique continues to be outbound currency smuggling, alongwith electronic transfers, Mexican bank drafts and the parallel Peso exchange market. Corruption remains the chief impediments to Mexican's anti-laundering efforts."

Under the auspices of UNO, there is an international campaign to crack down on an essential component of the problem of money laundering. Now countries have enacted laws to prevent money laundering and allow closer scrutiny of suspect bank accounts of criminals.

Government of India has issued anti-money laundering guidelines before introduction of the Prevention of Money Laundering Bill in Parliament. Indian Bill embraces money laundering from drug-trafficking, terrorism, profits from prostitution, extortion, smuggled items like gold, diamond etc. India's security is threatened by the spread of international crime control, free trade, globalization and advances in telecommunications leading to the increased reach of crime syndicates. The Bill in Section 3 deals with the offense of money laundering which states that whenever a person acquires, owns, possesses or transfers any proceeds of crime or knowingly enters into any transactions or deals or aids the concealment of the "proceeds of crime", means any property derived or obtained, directly or indirectly, by any person as a result of criminal activity relating to a scheduled offence or the value of such property. The Bill has the schedule offence which lists 16 sections of Indian Penal Code, 6 sections of Arms Act, 9 sections of Narcotic Drugs Act and 4 sections of the Prevention of Corruption Act. Thus the Bill covers all activities which are capable of producing illegal money. The Reserve Bank of India's panel has recommended rules against money laundering. According to the RBI's panel "The existing framework against money laundering activities in India needs further strengthening". This can be done by improving procedures and policies for preparing appropriate (banks) customer profiles and coordination and cooperation with regulatory and other authorities. The panel said banks operating in India should ascertain the source of funds in deposit schemes offered to expatriate Indians as part of their drive to prevent money laundering. It also suggested each bank appoint an anti-money laundering compliance officer and create profiles of customers. It called for creation of a data bank of suspicious transactions, which could then be circulated to banks to help them defect patterns of suspicious behaviours. However, the REI did not say when it intends to implement the recommendations. But technological initiatives in the Indian banking space have gradually gathered momentum ever since REI announced the policy of privatization of banking in 1993. Infrasoft Technologies has launched a money laundering software in India on the 17th of September, 2003. This is a huge development being India's first globally of adoptable Anti Money Laundering (AML) Software named OMNI Enterprise. Considering the size and dimension of the problem, and the alarm, Infrasoft Technologies, a specialist banking product player, is counting on its early mover advantage to make the lead way in the anti-money laundering products sphere that is estimated to be worth close to US$ 10 billion.

The United States has desired India to play a more aggressive role in its global campaign against terrorism and terrorist financing by joining groups striving to curb money laundering. The Indian

Parliament is yet to pass the Prevention of Money Laundering Bill, 1999, and the country is yet to join the Paris based Financial Action Task Force consisting of 29 nations which was set up in 1989 to prevent international money laundering. Since the September 11 attack, cutting off money to terrorists has topped the agenda of FATF, which includes the United States, Britain, Canada, France, Brazil and Switzerland. The panel has used FATF rules as a guideline. Alarmed with reports of money from global terrorist organizations flowing into their account, banks across the globe are implementing special anti-money laundering software to detect unusual flow of money.

CHAPTER 4 IT FRAUDS

FREQUENTLY USED CYBER CRIMES

Logic bombs

These are event dependent programs. This implies that these programs are created to do something only when a certain event (known as a trigger event) occurs. E.g. even some viruses may be termed logic bombs because they lie dormant all through the year and become active only on a particular date (like the Chernobyl virus).

Trojan attacks

A Trojan as this program is aptly called, is an unauthorized program which functions from inside what seems to be an authorized program, thereby concealing what it is actually doing.

There are many simple ways of installing a Trojan in someone's computer. To cite and example, two friends Rahul and Mukesh (names changed), had a heated argument over one girl, Radha (name changed) whom they both liked. When the girl, asked to choose, she chose Mukesh over Rahul, Rahul decided to get even. On the 14th of February, he sent Mukesh a spoofed e-card, which appeared to have come from Radha's mail account. The e-card actually contained a Trojan. As soon as Mukesh opened the card, the Trojan was installed on his computer. Rahul now had complete control over Mukesh's computer and proceeded to harass him thoroughly.

Internet time thefts

This connotes the usage by an unauthorized person of the Internet hours paid for by another person. In a case reported before the enactment of the Information Technology Act, 2000 Colonel Bajwa, a resident of New Delhi, asked a nearby net cafe owner to come and set up his Internet connection. For this purpose, the net cafe owner needed to know his username and password. After having set up the connection he went away with knowing the present username and password. He then sold this information to another net cafe. One week later Colonel Bajwa found that his Internet hours were almost over. Out of the 100 hours that he had bought, 94 hours had been used up within the span of that week. Surprised, he reported the incident to the Delhi police. The police could not believe that time could be stolen. They were not aware of the concept of time-theft at all. Colonel Bajwa's report was rejected. He decided to approach *The Times of India*, New Delhi. They, in turn carried a report about the inadequacy of the New Delhi Police in handling cyber crimes. The Commissioner of Police, Delhi then took the case into his own hands and the police under his directions raided and arrested the net cafe owner under the charge of theft as defined by the Indian Penal Code. The net cafe owner spent several weeks locked up in Tihar jail before being granted bail.

Web Hacking

This occurs when someone forcefully takes control of a website (by cracking the password and later changing it). The actual owner of the website does not have any more control over what appears on that website. In a recent incident reported in the USA the owner of a hobby website for children received an e-mail informing her that a group of hackers had gained control over her website. They demanded a ransom of 1 million dollars from her. The owner, a schoolteacher, did not take the threat seriously. She felt that it was just a scare tactic and ignored the e-mail. It was three days later that she came to know, following many telephone calls from all over the country, that the hackers had web jacked her website. Subsequently, they had altered a portion of the website which was titled 'How to have fun with goldfish'. In all the places where it had been mentioned, they had replaced the word 'goldfish' with the word 'piranhas'. Piranhas are tiny but extremely dangerous flesh-eating fish. Many children had visited the popular website and had believed what the contents of the website suggested. These unfortunate children followed the instructions, tried to play with piranhas, which they bought from pet shops, and were very seriously injured!

Theft of computer system

This type of offence involves the theft of a computer, some part(s) of a computer or a peripheral attached to the computer.

Physically damaging a computer system

This crime is committed by physically damaging a computer or its peripherals.

Internet fraud

The term 'Internet fraud' refers to any type of fraud scheme that uses email, web sites, chat rooms or message boards to present fraudulent solicitations to prospective victims, to conduct fraudulent transactions or to transmit the proceeds of fraud to financial institutions or to others connected with the scheme.

Some forms of Internet fraud, include:

- Spam
- Scams
- Spyware
- Identity theft

- Phishing
- Internet banking fraud

Spam

Spam is a generic term used to describe electronic 'junk mail' or unwanted messages sent to your email account or mobile phone. These messages vary, but are essentially commercial and often annoying in their sheer volume. They may try to persuade you to buy a product or service, or visit a website where you can make purchases; or they may attempt to trick you into divulging your bank account or credit card details.

More information about spam is available from the Australian Communications and Media Authority (ACMA website)

Scams

The power of the Internet and email communication has made it all too easy for email scams to flourish. These schemes often arrive uninvited by email. Many are related to the well-documented Nigerian Scam or Lotto Scams and use similar tactics in one form or another.

While the actual amount of money lost by businesses and the community is unknown, the number of people claiming to have been defrauded by these scams is relatively low.

More information about scams is available from the Australian Competition and Consumer Commission (ACCC) SCAMwatch website and the Australian Securities and Investments Commission FIDO website.

Spyware

Spyware is generally considered to be software that is secretly installed on a computer and takes things from it without the permission or knowledge of the user. Spyware may take personal information, business information, bandwidth; or processing capacity and secretly gives it to someone else. It is recognised as a growing problem.

More information about taking care of spyware is available from the Department of Broadband, Communication, and the Digital Economy (DBCDE) website.

Identity theft

A large part of online crime is now centred on identity theft which is part of identity fraud and specifically refers to the theft and use of personal identifying information of an actual person, as opposed to the use of a fictitious identity. This can include the theft and use of identifying personal information of persons either living or dead.

More information about how to prevent and respond to identity theft is available from the Attorney-General's Department website.

Phishing

Phishing is a technique used to gain personal information for the purpose of identity theft. Phishing involves using a form of spam to fraudulently gain access to people's online banking details. As well as targeting online banking customers, phishing emails may target online auction sites or other online payment facilities. Typically, a phishing email will ask an online banking customer to follow a link in order to update personal bank account details. If the link is followed, the victim downloads a program which captures his or her banking login details and sends them to a third party.

More information about phishing is available from the Australian High Tech Crime Centre (AHTCC) website.

FRAUD INVESTIGATION

Benefit Fraud Prevention/Detection

Torbay Council is very committed to tackling Benefit Fraud and has a number of tools to assist with these aims.

These include:

Use of Data Matching

This can indicate whether a Benefit Customer is concealing his true set of circumstances to a Local Authority. An example would be a customer who has started work, informed the Inland Revenue but failed to advise the Local Authority of this fact.

High Risk Interventions

The Department of Works and Pensions provides Local Authorities on a regular basis, details of claims that **may** be a risk to the local benefit system. These risks include Benefit Customers vacating addresses, starting work (or having increased earnings) and receiving undeclared Occupational Pensions.

The Department of Works and Pensions is continually developing products to identify customers who fail to declare changes in their circumstances and this in turn enables Local Authorities to identify potential benefit fraud.

Do Not Redirect Service

If a Benefit Customer vacates an address and fails to inform the Local Authority but places a redirection order on their post, all benefit related post to the customer is returned to the relevant Local Authority for further investigation.

Joint Working/Liaison with the Department for Work & Pensions (DWP)

The Investigations Team works closely with their opposite numbers in the DWP as many allegations involve both Housing/ Council Tax Benefit and DWP administered benefits such as Income Support and Income Based Job Seekers Allowance. The exchange of information between the offices is very important when carrying out enquiries. A joint exercise can very often have positive results that would not have been achieved by any organisation working in isolation.

Surveillance

Local Authorities are able to use surveillance in appropriate cases, however this has to be undertaken in accordance with the law and has to be authorised.

Authorised Officer Powers

Local Authorities are able to obtain employment details and other information benefit fraudsters attempt to conceal, by using this legislation.

1. The Government has set up the Serious Fraud Investigation Office (SFIO) under the Department of Company Affairs, Minstry of Finance to professionally investigate white-collar crimes vide Resolution No. 45011/16/2003-Admn I dated 2nd July 2003,
2. In continuation of the aforesaid Resolution, the responsibilities and functions of the SFIO will include, but not be limited to, the following:-
   a) The SFIO is expected to be a multi-disciplinary organization consisting of experts in the field of accountancy, forensic auditing, law, information technology, investigation, company law, capital market and taxation for detecting and prosecuting or recommending for prosecution white-collar crimes/ frauds.
   b) The SFIO will normally take up for investigation only such cases, which are characterized by –
      i) complexity and having inter-departmental and multi disciplinary ramifications
      ii) substantial involvement of public interest to be judged by size, either in terms of monetary misappropriation or in terms of persons affected, and;

iii) the possibility of investigation leading to or contributing towards a clear improvement in systems, laws or procedures.

c) The SFIO shall investigate serious cases of fraud received from Department of Company Affairs. SFIO may also take up cases on its own, subject to para (d) below. The SFIO would make investigation under the provisions of the Companies Act, 1956 and would also forward the investigation reports on violations of the provisions of other acts to the concerned agencies, for prosecution/appropriate action.

d) Whether or not an investigation should be taken up by the SFIO would be decided by the Director SFIO, who will be expected to record the reasons in writing. These decisions will be further subject to review by a coordination committee which has been constituted vide Order No. 5/15/2003-SFIO dated 16.04.2005.

3. The Director, SFIO has already been designated Head of the Department for financial and administrative purposes.

4. SFIO is expected to be set up as a modal office with state of the art facilities.

5. It may outsource work to professional agencies, on case to case basis, subject to the condition of compliance of relevant rules of the Government.

(b) CYBER MAFIA

Beware someone is lurking in your personal computer (P.C.) It is reported that your value in the cyber mafia –run chor –bazar has been prevalent. Your official name value is 0.25$, 2$ is for cell No., 150$ to 500$ for credit card No., 50$ to 400$ for bank customer ID and PIN. You could be worth $1000, on an average. When it comes to dealing in corporate information, your value could run into thousand of dollars. If fun and fame were the sole aim of cyber hijackers till some time ago, making fast buck is the key motive of today's cyber crackers. These nerds can outsmart tracker king Kevin David Mitnick. The tech savyness attached to the profession makes it proliferate in terms of value and volume.

How does one fall prey to the cyber mafia? The case of a Chandigarh bank executive says it all. He logged on to social networking site, a couple of months ago. Soon he started receiving mails from unknown sources asking about his health, and home loan details. He thought someone who knows him well was playing a prank, until a tech savvy friend realized that his computer has been hijacked and turned into a BOT (a hijack computer) a captive.

In the above case, when he logged on, a malware/spyware was downloaded into his system which held his computer a captive and started sending the entire data to an outsider exposing his passwords. Over 10,000 computers are converted into BOTs a day and are linked into large networks of such computers, called BOT nets. On an average around 400 BOTs are created a day in India according to recent study. The country has over 40 command and control servicer having 38465 distinct BOTs. Among the cities Mumbai reported a share of 33%, followed by Delhi at 25%, Chennai 17% and Bangalore 13%.

Handling malicious hackers

Imagine this. A hacker crates a look-alike site of a well-known bank. He sends across emails to customers requesting for confidential information claiming the bank's website is undergoing a revamp or reconstruction. The email has link embedded in it, which by default directs the customer to the fake site that the hacker has created. The customer, thinking it to be a genuine communication from the bank, provides the details which the hacker saves and later uses for fraudulent transactions such as money transfers or procuring critical passwords.

Not a secure situation to be in. The rapid growth of online commerce has brought increasing sophistication in internet fraud across multiple access channels. Threats from phishing (criminally fraudulent process of attempting to acquire sensitive information such as usernames, passwords and credit card details, by masquerading as a trustworthy entity in an electronic communication), pharming (a hacker's attack aiming to redirect a website's traffic to another, bogus website), Trojans (type of malicious software), key logging (useful to retrieve online password entries by capturing keyboard strokes), and proxy attacks, combined with regulation and mandates (HIPAA, PCI) governing online data piracy, place online security at a premium.

To thwart hackers, banks are adopting stringent levels of login procedures, which are more personalized and secure. Some of them include the introduction of additional levels of passwords, personalized back-ground image for login or virtual keyboards. For instance, to prevent keylogging, financial transaction sites are installing virtual keypads and virtual mouse. As part of the login process, while a bank designs its normal login password—instead of typing that password on the keyboard – the user will be able to use the cursor to select his/her password on the virtual keyboard. This process will circumvent the key locking setup enforced by the hacker.

While user access has been established, it is equally important to prevent frauds and enable real time risk assessment. Online fraud detection requires the use of multiple IT security tools. It needs to be able to evaluate risk by anlysing data from variety of sources, including profiles, device fingerprints, IP and other network forensics data, geo-location information, and transactional data. By bringing together various risk factors in a single policy a well-implemented solution can score the relative risk of a transaction, proactively prevent fraud and instantly alert the organization to threats. Such technology provides real time and offline risk analysis to maximize the efficiency of capturing and analyzing real-time transaction data, matching the risk profile of the current transaction against historical patterns.

The define and refine fraud prevention policy, investigation and forensic tools are also needed to simplify inherently difficult administrative tasks such as policy authoring, risk monitoring, incident investigation or audit data analysis. Information technology gives security administrators the ability to experiment with different security policies (without having to bring down a production system) and adopt tools best suited for their organistions.

So companies can minimize the chances of letting anyone use a stolen credit card for multiple, fictitious transactions like flight bookings or online purchase or even financial or trading requests. As companies aggressively embrace the internet for sales self-service and information sharing, online security is crucial to establishing trust between companies and users.

A recent online security survey from a cross-section of India's top 40 banks by Readi Minds State of Online Security in Financial Institution in India-2008 has reported that 30% of banks have been victims of identify theft during the last one year, while 30% of the banks have been victims of phishing at the same time.

Online security has become a business issue. There seems to be a strong link between the business performance of a financial institution and the online security measures implemented by it. Over 70% of banks that reported to have implemented strong security also regularly deliver better business performance compared to their peer group. But the worrying issue was that over 57% of banks still do not have a dedicated budget for online security. Online security is still part of the IT budget. But the good part of the finding was that 100% of respondents were aware that integrating stronger user authentication, with fraud detection, and risk-based transaction verification is the strongest form of defence against online identity theft and financial frauds.

The Identity and Access Management (IAM) software market as one of the fastest growing security software markets in Asia Pacific, is growing at a compounded annual growth rate (CAGR) of 17% (2008-2012) to reach $524 million by 2012.

E-crime trail

When cyber forensics expert and his team were asked to review the entire IT infrastructure of a pharmaceutical firm, many officials within the company saw it as a waste of time. The pharma major had enough indications that sensitive drug development related information was being electronically leaked out of the company. While analysing the company's IT systems, expert found that one of the company's main servers was exceptionally 'well hardened' while the others were not. (In computing, hardening is usually the process of securing a system. This work is especially done to protect systems against attackers and would typically include removal of unnecessary user names or logins and the disabling of unnecessary services.) This convinced that the systems engineer could not have done it on his own if he had done it, a similar degree of sophistication would have shown in his work with the other servers. After several rounds of questioning the systems engineer confessed that one of his Internet chat friends gave him tips to secure that particular server. Though the engineer's answer was satisfactory, expert could smell a rat. Right in the heart of the server resided an information-stealing Trojan virus, which would capture all the internal mails sent between the company R&D officials and send multiple copies of the same to multiple e-mail IDs through the Internet. And the Trojan made its way into the server through a series of seemingly safe software files exchanged between the systems engineer and his chat friend. Since the Internet friend did not want the crime to easily come to light, he ensured that his protege secured the system beyond comprehension.

The investigation of a computer system, mobile phone, iPod, Wi-Fi networks or any other digital device that is believed to be involved in a cyber crime is called cyber forensics, e-forensics or digital forensics. Given the multi-fold rise in cyber crimes, there has been a spurt in demand for cyber forensics experts. A cyber forensic expert is expected to be capable enough to retrieve any kind of information from these device even if it has been destroyed, deleted or corrupted. If the hard disk of a computer has crashed, there is 95 per cent chance of it being recovered through various e-forensics tools. And he has a host of hardware and software enablers, some of which are researched on and developed at the Thiruvananthapuram-based Centre for Development of Advanced Computing (C-DAC). Digital forensics is something that is highly misunderstood by the common man. The general notion is that breaking into a network or an IT system is what e-forensics is all about. As a discipline, e-forensics started gaining importance roughly five years ago with the increase in broadband penetration in the country. Today, technology is increasingly being used for corporate spying, espionage and for spreading terror. If a top official resigns from a large company, it is common practice these days to get that official's official laptop, PC and official mobile phone analysed by a bunch of cyber experts. This is basically to ascertain whether the official has been passing on sensitive company-specific information to competitors. Many top companies have their own security solution divisions. With terrorists and anti-social elements becoming more tech savvy than ever, the country requires an army of such experts who can crack the code once a cyber crime has been committed. According to some estimates, there is a shortage of about 20,000 cyber forensics officials in the country. It may be noted that after the recent arrest of Mansur Peerbhoy, the techie from Pune who was allegedly responsible for sending threatening e-mails prior to the serial blasts in Ahmedabad and Delhi, his laptop, the CPU of his personal computer and office work station were seized by the police. This would have helped the police generate a couple of other interesting leads, says the e-forensics scientist. By implementing something called eMail Tracer, the police can understand where the terror mail originated from. It can also reveal how many people were a part of this e-chain. Moreover, as mentioned earlier, all files that were ever created or received on the person's hard disk could be retrieved, according to the scientists. Generally, officers from the various cyber crime cells of the police work on such cases. However, due to the spurt in the number of cyber crimes happening in India, the police do outsource many of the functions to third party companies. On the other hand, corporates are very sceptical of approaching the police even if they fear a cyber crime has been committed on their systems. In many cases, the business critical servers and hardware have to be deposited with the police. No company would want the continuity of its business to be impacted and hence they prefer to first talk to third party cyber forensic experts. The modus operandi is to understand what has gone wrong and then approach the police, if required.

Precautions to be taken

A good e-forensics expert should be able to think like a criminal; yet be better than a criminal. This profession calls for a high degree of analytics skills as interpreting evidence wrongly could mislead everyone. Any average techie would have been fooled by, seeing the security level of the hardened, server. It was the 'out of the box' analytical thinking on expert part that helped the pharma company stem the loss of critical information.

A cyber forensics professional could hail from diverse backgrounds such as IT, law or even common business. However, he needs to have some experience of working in an architected system and an enterprise wide system. Knowledge of telecom and knowhow of the loopholes in security paradigms are very crucial. 'Today, a qualified e-forensics professional could either work with the police, third party agencies or with corporates. "I know of companies such as Infosys, Satyam and Deloitte Consulting who prefer having such people on board rather than going in for outside help," the e-forensics expert says. The starting salary for professionals in this space is double that of an average software programmer. "If somebody has very specific high end skill-set, we would not mind giving him Rs 30,000-Rs 40,000 per month. Unlike the IT or BPO industry, this is an area where there is no slowdown. For recovering a hard disk alone, self employed e-forensics professionals are known to charge upto Rs 15,000. However, experts lament the absence of a proper ecosystem to foster talent in this space. First, there are only a handful of institutions that teach such courses. The University of Madras, C-DAC, Indian Institute of Information Technology (Allahabad) are some of the known names in this space. Apart from this there are several organisations that provide five-to-10-day crash courses. "Very few of these short-term courses are of a holistic nature. At best, they would teach how to do penetration testing. A penetration test is a method of evaluating the security of a computer system or network by simulating an attack by a malicious user.

Some IT security experts are of the view that there is not enough legislation in India to enable e-forensics to flourish as a fullfledged science.

In spite of enacting the Information Technology Act in 2000 the judiciary is yet to create rules that would help quicken the legal process and set norms related to the seizure of electronic evidence. If courts take upto 20 years to decide on a case, how are you going to keep the digital evidence live and valid for that period?

There are glaring loopholes in our revised cyber laws

The IT Amendment Bill 2008, which has been passed by the Lok Sabha and Rajya Sabha in the last week of December 2008, aims to make sweeping changes in the existing Indian cyber law Framework.

Due credit needs to be given to the government, for removing the various practical difficulties of the IT Act, 2000.

Issues related to confidential information and data of corporations — and their adequate protection — have not been adequately addressed. The said law is not a comprehensive law on data protection or on digital secrets. Having a couple of sections on data protection does not serve the requirements of corporate India.

India has neither learnt from America's or the European Union's experiences in the area of data protection. The proposed provisions will not aid victim entities, whose data and information is often misused by their employees — or their agents — with impunity.

The IT Act amendments are also deficient in the sense that they do not create rebuttable presumptions of confidentiality of trade secrets and information. A large number of companies and individuals today save their confidential data, information and trade secrets in the electronic form on their computers. Given the apparent increase in the adoption of technology, it is increasingly being found that despite all precautions, the employees are still going ahead and taking away confidential data from companies.

The inability of the law to create enabling presumptions of confidentiality regarding corporate and individual data and information in the electronic form is likely to complicate matters further for Indian companies and netizens. Given the move to make most cyber crimes bailable offences, corporations can forget about being able to get their errant employees, who misuse confidential data and information, behind bars.

Absence of an effective remedy for corporations is likely to further erode the confidence of the industry in the new cyber-legal regime. The maximum damage by way of compensation stipulated by the new cyber law amendments is Rs 5 crore. When calculated in dollar terms, this is a small figure and hardly provides any effective relief to corporations, whose confidential information, which might be worth several crores, is stolen or misused by its employees.

Another major failure of the proposed amendments is that they have not addressed the issue of spam in a comprehensive manner. The word spam is not even mentioned anywhere in the IT Amendment Bill. India has missed yet another opportunity to deal with the contentious issue. It is pertinent to note that countries like the US, Australia and New Zealand have demonstrated their intention to fight spam by putting in place a dedicated anti-spam legislation. This lacuna is all the more serious since India already features among the top 10 nations in the world, from where spam originates.

Today, people and organisations are increasingly relying upon electronic evidence and electronic media as a means of communicating with each other and doing business. However the amendments are completely silent on the issues of electronic discovery. This once again shows up the short-sightedness of those who have designed the amendments.

The amendments to the IT Act do not address jurisdictional issues. At a time when internet has made geography history, it was hoped that the new amendments would throw light on complicated issues pertaining to jurisdiction. This is because numerous activities on internet take place in different jurisdictions. There is a need to enable Indian authorities to get jurisdiction over data and information impacting India in a more comprehensive manner.

The new amendments make it mandatory for corporations possessing, dealing or handling any sensitive personal data or information in a computer resource to maintain reasonable security practices and procedures. However, what these "reasonable security practices and procedures" would be is anybody's guess. It has to be pointed out that one set of security practices will not fit the entire nation. What would be reasonable security practices for one industry may not be applicable to another industry. Not maintaining such security practices would expose corporations to civil liability and they would have to cough up compensation to the affected person to the tune of Rs 5 crore.

The new amendments are likely to impact all industries which use computers, computer systems and networks, and data and information in electronic form.

Cyber Crime

These days menace of cyber crime is growing and precautions are required to be taken by both individual users and organizations to protect themselves from such crime. Besides traditional cyber crime like identity theft and inducing people to pay for imaginary services and non-existent goods, a new ingenious variant to it now came from different kind of individuals and groups. Now the organized gangs have entered in cyber crime having realized that it is much more profitable than routine crime and could be executed with greater ease and less chance of being caught. For example a lawyer assembled a group of 300 persons from different walks of life and skills and hijacked computers at will to convert them into 'Botnets', which were later used for many illegal ventures. Similarly a virtual group in US entered into systems and got hold of Credit Cards details involving 25 million transactions which were then diverted to Ukraine, which were later used to buy larger quantities of goods and sold on e-Bay.

New arrivals in cyber crime include a substantial numbers who are destructive and get pleasure from disrupting normal life. The semi-skilled having half backed knowledge cause damage to a system. Net is extremely vulnerable to mischief that is mostly inadvertent or innocuous which occasionally take the form of a deliberate and malicious attack bordering on crime. There is rising cyber hostilities arising from animosity between nations. The conflicts between Georgia and Russia have witnessed the same phenomenon with many computers in the former country becoming an easy target for attacks emanating from across the border. In India also the attacks possibly originating from Pakistan defaces the many web-sites. Fortunately this type of cyber crime is at present at nascent stage, not yet waged into cyber war.

To eliminate crime on web, absolute totalitarian control is required. Experts advocated at the Davos Economic Summit about the requirement of concerted promotion of a civic spirit amongst net users, akin to the open source software movement with transparency and hallmark of the net.

CHAPTER 5 CRIMINAL CASES

SCARLETT KEELING CASE

Scarlett Eden Keeling was drugged, raped and left to die in shallow waters on Goa's popular Anjuna beach on Feb. 18th 2008. Two locals were arrested in the case.

The NCW (National Commission for Women) has said, Goa cops investigations into the rape and murder of Scarlett Keeling are completely misleading. From the beginning police have destroyed evidence. They have spoiled the case and there are big lapses in the investigation. They suspected foul play in investigation inasmuch as one of the important evidences LUI Cafe and temporary shack where Scarlett spent her last moment, had been removed. Cops should have safeguarded if for the sake of the investigation. The NCW members also questioned the authenticity of viscera report from the forensic laboratory in Kalina Mumbai. Viscera was sent for examination by Goa cops after a month. Prima facie it appeared to be tampered. Further they said, "after going through Scarlett's photograph taken soon after her body was found on Anjuna Beach in the morning of February 18th they have come to the conclusion that the brutal crime was committed by more than three men. While one man probably injected morphine into her back, another tried to silence her, the third one squeezed her and the fourth must have raped her and then drowned her". The British teenager's rape and murder rocked the tourist destination, with the first autopsy saying it was a case of drowning. However the second post-mortem suggested the case should be treated as homicide. The forensic experts say Scarlett was raped and murdered. However, her mother Fiona wanted to conduct another forensic test before performing the last rites.

It is reported that under pressure on the credibility of police probe, the state Government has handed over the case of death of British teenager Scarlett Eden Keeling to the CBI. Scarlett's mother, Fiona Mackeown, had sought CBI inquiry into her death and alleged cover up by the police. Rubbishing the allegation of cover-up, the Government announced that "there are no moves to hush up and no attempt to hide anything in the case". Fiona had alleged that there is drug trade links in the impugned case. The Government while refusing the opposition highlighted drug trade and deterioting law and order situation in the coastal state said that there was a sustained campaign to spoil Goa's name to harm the tourism industry. Isolated incidence like this happen all over the world but a systematic campaign was being carried against the state for over 20 days by the media and urged to take a united stand to protect the state interest.

The Scarlett Keeling case has received a great deal of attention. In Rajya Sabha, there was a sharp exchange of views on the case. A view expressed in Parliament that it was the responsibility of parents to take care of the security of their children finds resonance among some people. Indeed, the Goa government and its spokespersons have projected the case as a tragedy caused by bad parenting. They have said that if the mother had been more responsible, if the victim had been a "good girl", then...

Whatever opinions one might hold on the issue of parenting, they are of little relevance to the case, except as a cover for a ghastly crime of rape and murder committed on a young woman. Fiona Mackeown may be a very bad mother, but it was her single-minded determination and courage to uncover the truth behind her daughter's death that forced a second post mortem and revealed the ugly face of sexual violence behind Scarlett's death.

Although we know the details of the lives of Scarlett and her family ferreted out by an insatiable media, it is striking that there is little known about the antecedents of the criminals. Who are they, what was their parenting? Day after day in rural India young girls from poor families, run the risk of inviting unwanted attention from sons of the rural elite, often becoming the victims of rape and murder. In all such cases the issue of parenting disappears in the culture of "boys will be boys". What about the issue of parenting when sons of the rich and famous throw their weight around, get involved in drunken brawls and abuse and sexually harass women? Do we dare to put their parents out on display and ask them deeply invasive questions as to what went wrong with them as parents.

Parenting is important and parental negligence can have disastrous consequences. It is normal for parents to dream that their children do well. But the bottom line in a case of rape and murder of a young woman is that the victim and her family must get justice. The issue of parenting in this case is a substitute for the crude ignorance and bigoted opinions women face when they complain of sexual harassment. This is not necessarily from the cop on the street but often from those holding high constitutional office.

For a victim of sexual harassment the first battle is to go public with a complaint. It takes enormous courage to do so. Character assassination of the victim is often the norm used by the defence. Recently, the chief justice of a southern state reportedly made the horrifying comment that "nowadays women wear such kind of dresses even in temples and churches that when we go to places of worship, instead of meditating on God, we end up meditating on the person in front of us". Can such a learned person be expected to do justice to a woman victim appearing before him? Would it not be appropriate for women in the state to demand that he recuse himself from every case concerning sexual violence against women?

Or take this statement from the head of a state human rights commission. He reportedly said about a sexual harassment case on New Year's eve in Mumbai: "Yes men are bad. But who asked them (women) to venture out at night... Women should not venture out at night and when they do there is no point in complaining that men touched them and hit them. If this is not an invitation for sexual harassment, then what is?" We are hypocritical in the extreme, about our attitudes towards women. The rot often begins at the top. There should be a gender-sensitive index used against such persons who can influence the processes of justice whether in the courts, the administrative machinery, the police force or our legislatures.

Crimes against women, and specifically crimes against minors, are increasing. In the capital, two-thirds of rape victims are minors, yet the conviction rates are extremely low. Negative attitudes towards the victim also tend to influence the processes of justice. We need to support the victim and, in the cases of rape and murder, her family. Scarlett's rapist and killers must be caught and punished. The role of drug-pushing networks, should be investigated. It would be a travesty of justice if judgments on social behaviour are impacted on the follow-up of the case.

(b) NITHARI KILLINGS: THE ROAR OF A CANNIBAL

The year 2006 goes by and two psychopaths smirk in the aftermath of sin. What screams for justice is a heinous slaying, a nerve raking cold-blooded murder in the name of fate: 19 killings seem to have withered in the fog of time.

The narrow dwindling lanes of an impoverished neighbourhood in Noida stand overlooking a sophisticated colony. Who could have known that Kothi number D-5 was the house of several corpses? Owned by Noida-based businessman Moninder Singh

Pandher, the Kothi was nothing less than a slaughterhouse for innocent children and women who stepped out of their homes not knowing that they were never going to return. If we rewind the time year back, we cannot forget that day when the gruesome Nithari killings came to light from a dirty drain in Noida. There was a sense of overwhelming evil at the crime scene as bits of bone, plastic bags full of entrails, children's body parts, skulls, shoes, tiffin boxes and bits of clothing were dug out.

The ghoulish killings were carried out by Surendra Koli, Pandher's domestic help allegedly a cannibal and a necrophiliac. For several months the decomposed remains of the chilling murders were dug from the hellish pit. The raped and murdered children and women screamed for justice. The moments when they were being tortured and cast into a living hell cannot be expressed in words but they certainly cannot go unnoticed in the name of a weak administration, careless system and greedy investigation.

According to the alleged, Surender Koli, "I used to kill only women and children —mostly girls. It was as if I'd go out of my senses. I couldn't even recall anything later. I'd call the victim and ask her if she was looking for work or lure a kid with a smile or some nice words. Then I'd kill my victim and try to have sex with them. Then I'd take them to the bathroom and cut their body in pieces and throw them behind the house. I'd even cook the flesh at times and eat it." According to psychiatrist: "A deep rooted scar or a certain incident in the past can trigger such instances. We are living in a society where cannibalism is considered to be abnormal. People like Koli are potentially dangerous to the society. What he did is a gruesome act and no one in their right mind would even think about such a thing." A housewife, opines: "I am really scared for my children after the Nithari killings came to light. I dismissed both my male domestic helps and have now settled in for a lady who was known to my mother in the village. It is very difficult for one to say anything about anyone these days. I am so scared that I don't let my children step out of the house after 5:30 in the evening."

It has been a year since the Nithari killings were revealed. The incident seemed to have taken the country by shock. But our authorities that seem to be sleeping most of the time are lazing around weary of hearing the pleas for help by grieving parents and relatives of those who were victimized. According to a report, out of 19 cases registered by the Central Bureau of Investigation (CBI) for the Nithari serial rapes and killings, the agency has completed its investigations in 11. Pandher has been given a clean chit in 10 cases having been indicted only for one—soliciting women for sex. In an interview, Koli had mentioned that Moninder often brought call girls home and that was what had triggered these killings. He had also stated that a couple of times he had given the cooked human flesh to Pandher as well. The judiciary might have given hope of justice to the mourning parents of the victims by framing charges of rape and murder against Pandher but on the other hand the CBI is facing charges that it was devastating the prosecution. The enraged parents brought to light the reality of our good old police force stating that even after visiting the police station a number of times, no complaint was registered about the missing children and women. This leads us to think what kind of system are we following as citizens and when will the time come for the authorities to wake up? A grieving father says, "I went to the police station to get my complaint filed. They did not entertain me. They said that if they found my child they would get back to me." The police seem to have treated the matter rather lightly. This has further triggered discontent in the minds of the people of Nithari. In Payal's case (victim), the CBI had filed its first charge sheet in Ghaziabad releasing Pandher and charging Koli with the crime despite being aware of the confessions given by Pandher and Koli in the initial probe by the Noida police that both of them were equal partners in the crime. Arjun Khetripal, businessman says, " If Pandher is one of the criminals and the CBI defends him for money or anything else, how safe will it be for a serial killer to be on the lose? It might happen that a few years down the line when everybody forgets about the Nithari killings, he ends up murdering few more innocent children."

Neharika Modi, ombudsperson, says, "The Nithari killings should be an eye opener for our government and authorities. The murderer is on the prowl and no one is ready to do anything about it. The grieving parents want justice. They want the two to be hanged and why not? How safe would it be for two cannibals to be defended? If a tiger becomes a man-eater, we shoot it. Here we are talking about the psychology of the human brain that can think, plan and conduct." There was sufficient evidence to prosecute Pandher on charges of rape and murder in four cases.

Pinki Sarkar's father drowned in the Ganges in Behrampur in Murshidabad district in West Bengal under mysterious circumstances. His wife moved the Supreme Court alleging that the CBI was behind this and that her husband was getting constant threats to withdraw his charges against Pandher. The nation watches on, as the parents of the murdered await justice. What will be the final outcome of Nithari killings? This is one question that has been boggling the minds of thousands of parents and children all across the country. A bloodthirsty pair of eyes might be following a child somewhere, the next moment there would be an empty swing creaking in an isolated playground with boiled body parts being served on someone's dining table.

In Nithari killings the main accused was declared innocent. It is reported that the CBI has again freed the main accused Mohinder Singh Pandhar from the charge of kidnapping and murder of a 10-year-old girl child.

Judicial magistrate Smt. Sapna Mishra has declared Pandhar innocent in the 12th charge sheet filed by the CBI in the case of murder of a girl named Nisha. However the CBI has claimed that the servant of Pandhar, Surinder Koli is the main accused in the case. The court has admitted the charge sheet. Before this in all the charge sheets filed by the CBI, the court has declared Mohinder Singh innocent except in the case of murder of Payal.

Nithari Case

At least one chapter of the Nithari serial rapes and killings has ended on a positive note. More than two years after the killing, Mohinder Singh Pandher along with his servant Surinder Koli was convicted and sentenced to death penalty in rare of rarest case for kidnapping, raping and murder of 14 years old Rimpa Haldhar, besides chopping up and hiding her body in the drain. She used to work at Pandher's house and was found missing on Feb 5, 2005. The decision of the court has come in one of the 19 cases filed in the court. The investigating agency CBI has stated at the beginning that there is no direct evidence against Mohinder Singh. The accused may prefer appeal in the case. Judiciary has done a commendable job and has shown some light to the investigating agencies.

(c) SHIVANI BHATNAGAR CASE

This is a case of conviction for premeditated murder. *Quis custodiet ipsos custodes*—who will guard us from the guards themselves? Was the querry posed by the philosopher Juvenal in ancient Rome while stating that the gravity of a heinous offence was compounded manifold when it was committed by a person appointed to prevent crime. One wonders what Juvenal would have said if he had been present on March 24, 2008 in the Delhi Civil Court when additional session Judge R.K. Shastri observed that premediated murder of scribe Shivani Bhatnagar was not an offence of the kind which could shock the conscious of society and went on to press the main accused – suspended IG of police R.K. Saxena — of having an excellent service record and of being an asset to the nation, except for the crime in question. While sentencing Sharma to life imprisonment the Judge took note of his service with the UN, Interpol, the PMO and CBI.

Prosecutor S.K. Saxena had sought death penalty for Sharma and his accomplice Pradeep who carried out the crime on Jan. 23 1999.

The prosecution held that this was "a premeditated act of cold blooded murder" which met the Supreme Court criterion that death penalty be awarded in " rarest of rare cases". Shivani was stabbed 39 times when she was alone in her apartment with her three months old baby who turned blue in the cold by the time the crime was discovered. The prosecution held that Sharma had passed on classified document to Shivani, that the two became intimate, and that when he started avoiding her, she threatened to expose him for leaking information. The defence council argued that "just because a journalist was allegedly killed by an IPS officer, it doesn't constitute an offence calling for maximum punishment." The contrary view could be that a good ACR (annual confidential report) is not a mitigating factor for premeditated murder just because the convict is a senior IPS officer.

(d) SANJAY DUTT CASE

Dutt's relationships weren't confined to the underworld. Investigating agencies and the prosecution maintain that they were under tremendous political pressure to go soft on him. On one occasion, while Special Public Prosecutor Ujjwal Nikam was arguing against Dutt's appeal for probation, CBI Chief Investigating Officer O.P. Chhatwal got a call on his mobile, and when he came back, he attempted to calm Nikam's impassioned plea to the court. One of the rumours doing the rounds among the Mumbai Police is that a telephone diary, which contained the numbers of many from the underworld, was recovered from Dubai. The number of Anees in the diary tallied with a number Dutt frequently called. But the diary never made it to the court as evidence.

Ironically, less than eight months, the same court had announced that Dutt was no terrorist, a development he treated as a certificate of good character from the judge. But justice as they say, is reason without passion, and Kode chose reason over emotion. While rejecting his plea for probation under the Probation of Offenders Act of 1958, the judge made it clear that while the court had accepted the fact that he had acquired the AK-56 for self-defence, it clearly wasn't Dutt's first offence. Said Kode: "His first offence was the acquisition of the 9 min pistol from one Kayyum, a key aide of Dawood, in September 1992. His second offence was the acquisition of the AK-56 and ammunition in January 1993, for which he has been held guilty under the Arms Act." Dutt already possessed three licenced weapons—a 375 Magnum double-barrelled rifle, a 12bore gun with double barrels, and a 270 Bruno rifle. "He had different types of licenced weapons, so where was the need for an AK-56 rifle, a weapon of mass destruction," questions Nikam.

Quoting his confession, the court traced his romance with the underworld back to the time when he was shooting for Firoz Khan's *Yalgaar* in Dubai in 1992. That was the first time Dutt met Dawood and attended parties thrown by him and his brother Anees. In his confession, Dutt clearly admits that he met Mirchi and Rajan in this period, something that has not worked in his favour.

After Dutt discovered that Magnum Videos' Samir Hingora and Hanif Kadawala had been arrested in connection with the Mumbai bomb blasts, he called Nulwala and asked him to destroy the weapons. "He advocated others to commit a crime, which is a very serious offence," Kode surmised. Nulwala picked up the arms from Dutt's Bandra residence and took them to Adajania, who owned a fabrication unit, and melted the AK-56 with a gas cutter. The duo agreed to deal with the pistol the next day. Since Adajania had to go to Kolkata the next day, he left the pistol with his friend Mulla. The court acknowledged that Mulla knew nothing about the conspiracy, and when Adajania failed to pick up the pistol after nine days, Mulla gave it to Ajay Marwah. Said Kode: "He was deceived by a friend and got embroiled in the case due to him". The judgment has come as a shock not just to Dutt's family, but to the entire film industry. His directors and co-stars alike believe that he has been given a very harsh sentence.

Sanjay Dutt's role in Mumbai bomb blasts is a case of confusion and punishment. The Special TADA judge P.D. Kode has lived and breathed the Mumbai blast case for the last 11 years and has at last completed his assignment of deciding the case. The sincere Kode, who has been holding court since 1996 in a high security makeshift building in one of the corridors of Arthur Road Jail, is nothing less than a workaholic who reportedly never missed a day of work before he slipped and fractured his arm in June 2007. He even attended his court on the day his farther died after disposing of his dead body. Though Kode sentenced Sanjay Dutt to 6 years imprisonment, the actor happily accepted the verdict and said, "you are like family to us".

It was a proud day for our judicial system that it did not get taken in by the huge wave of public sympathy for the movie star and the din of celebration which surrounded him. The wheels of justice ground slowly but surely. The serial bombings in Mumbai claimed 257 lives, and punishing the guilty has taken 14 years, 686 witness and 13000 pages of testimony. Sanjay Dutt is one of the 50 convicted who will serve between three and 14 years in Jail, with judge Kode sentencing 12 to death and 20 to a life behind bar.

The popular cine star and the film industry were shocked by the verdict but the judge made it clear that being a celebrity has no value when it comes to breaking the law. The judge observed "Sanjay Dutt was a mature man of 34 years when he committed the offence. He committed a chain of crime, acquiring such weapons (AK-56) shows scant respect for the law. It is an eminently dangerous act". He further stated, " your crime was not ghastly brutal, inhuman, or anti-social and did not result in harm to any one but still it is a serious offence and encourage others to break the law. Laws of the nation come first".

The life of movie star Sanjay Dutt has been full of contradictions and imitates. Sanjay went from being a problem child of the famous Bollywood couple Nargis and Sunil Dutt, to a main accused of a role in India's worst terrorist bombing, from a jail inmate to once again becoming a popular actor and then, back in jail as a convict. His life has been full of ironies also. After 16 months in jail for possessing illegal weapons, he was released on bail in 1995. In 12 years that followed, he became Bollywood's renaissance man. Sanjay Dutt rebuilt his carrier to a point where he was a bankable star again. He was associated not with the image of a public villain but with "Munna Bhai", the good hearted gangster of the underworld kind he was found guilty of associating with. The irony does not end there. In the even more successful Munnabhai sequel the character shared a mystical relationship with the spirit of Mahatma Gandhi and practiced Gandhigiri. All the while the shadow of the Mumbai blast case hung over Sanjay Dutt and finally the long arm of the law caught up with his soaring career. Bollywood stardom had allowed Dutt to ride over the blast case and resurrect his career. When he was acquitted of terror charges related to the bombings and the case taken out of the TADA court amidst some controversy, it was widely expected he would receive probation. But, putting the case completely into perspective, the judge P.D. Kode sentenced Sanjay to 6 year's rigorous imprisonment for possession of arms received from key accused. Kode stated that he could not treat Sanjay case as a minor offence and said, " Every one makes mistakes, but the element of criminality in you is incurable".

Chronology of Mumbai blast case

1. March 12, 1993 - 13 serial blasts rock the city of Mumbai.
2. April 13, 1993 - Samir Hingora and Hanif Kadawala arrested and they implicate Sanjay Dutt.
3. April 15, 1993 - Dutt chargesheeted for possessing arms, arrested on April 19.
4. Nov. 4, 1993 - 10,000 pages charge-sheet filed against 189 including Dutt.
5. Nov. 19, 1993 - Case handed over to the CBI

6. April 10, 1985	-	Charges dropped against 26, framed against the remaining
7. June 30, 1995	-	Accused duo Mohd. Jameel and Usman Jan Khan turn approvers
8. Oct 14, 1995	-	Sanjay Dutt granted bail by Supreme Court, released from the Mumbai Jail.
9. March 29, 1995	-	P.D. Kode made special TADA Judge after transfer of Judge J.N. Patil
10. Sept., 12 2006	-	Court begins delivering judgment on the case.

(e) MUMBAI BLAST CASE

The CBI's Chief Investigating officer O.P. Chhatwal calls it a "copybook case". Never before in criminal history has a chargesheet run into 10,000 pages. And never has any other trial seen 3,000 witnesses, 100 convictions, of which 12 are death penalties and 20 life sentences. Says Nikam, "When the case began, it was nearly impossible to establish where it started till we managed to turn two of the accused Mohammad Jameel and Mohammad Usman Jan Khan into approvers." The sentences have been given on the basis of the confessions of the accused and the co-accused, as the plot was hatched behind closed doors: in this case, the doors of Al-Hussaini Building, the residence of the Memons, the key conspirators. However, questions are being raised over the alleged pact between CBI and the Memon family. Rumours are rife that Yakub Memon made a deal whereby CBI was to be lenient to him if he cooperated. Chhatwal, however, denies this.

The Pakistan connection is clear from the confessions, with many of the approvers admitting to weapons training there. Says Nikam: "We have established that ISI was involved. The people who got weapons training were escorted by Pakistani officials from Dubai to Islamabad." Once the two accused started singing, the Mumbai Police and CBI put the plot into place. The conspiracy was spearheaded by Tiger Memon, who garnered the support of enraged Muslims after the fall of the Babri Masjid. Within weeks, over 170 people were rounded up and taken into custody and 27 cases were filed. The investigating agencies recovered arms and explosive material in 33 places in Maharashtra and elsewhere.

The most incriminating evidence was the Arches grenades, which were recovered in Mumbai. The grenades, which were part of the consignment that landed in Maharashtra prior to the blasts, were manufactured in Pakistan. Yet, despite ISI having provided weapons training to Indian Muslims with the intention of causing mass killing, charges of waging a war against India were dropped from the chargesheet in 1994. Chhatwal says, "Taking into consideration the law prevailing at that time and the ingredients of Section 121 of IPC, the prosecutors conducting the trial were of the view that this charge may not sustain and this was agreed upon by the designated court." Other investigating officers now admit dropping the charge was a mistake. The Supreme Court has, in other cases, held that acts of terrorism can amount to waging of war. In fact, Kode, while, announcing death sentences in connection with the Mahim fishermen colony blast, stated: "This is an offence of the highest degree and synonymous to waging war."

Though hearings in the trial had ended by September 2003, the case was in limbo till Abu Salem, former Dawood gang member and key accused, was extradited from Portugal in November 2005. With 100 out of the 123 who were tried being convicted, this is the highest conviction rate in any case. Maneshinde admits, "There is no precedent to this case, as never before have so many people been tried together, nor has the rate of conviction been so high."

(f) GODHARA RIOTS CASE

The Hon'ble Supreme Court's direction to the Gujarat Government to constitute a special investigation team (SIT) to reinvestigate the post Godhra communal riots and to submit the report within three months, was a welcome step. Even a larger communal polarization in the state is patently clear, and the administration of the state, under whose watch the riots occurred, has been seeking to present the image of a model state run by an efficient and able administrator. This image is belied by the fact that previous probes into the riots were a botched affair, not the least because of the state administration's willful attempts to thwart the investigation. The direction by the Supreme Court, even while not submitting to the constitutional norm of keeping law and order a state subject, presented a chance for the state machinery to redeem itself to whatever extent possible. Nonetheless, the Supreme Court move acknowledges the huge lacunae in the previous investigation. There are reasonable grounds to apprehend that attempts would be made to subvert the investigation. The SC remained vigilant of such efforts and not ruled out a CBI probe in case the SIT investigation becomes another inefficient exercise.

That a fair and transparent trial within the state is difficult, given the sheer hostility encountered by the witness, many of whom had turned hostile whether due to threats or inducements was also clear. Now the constitution of the SIT itself suggests that the trial of these cases might be shifted out of the state. Ensuring judicial remedy for the victims of the Gujrat riot of 2002 in which thousands were killed and injured, and lakhs displaced is critical for maintaining India's demographic and plausible ethos as well as an affirmation of the ability of our legal mechanism to deliver justice. The SIT probe is a step in the right direction.

(g) MOB VIOLENCE

Respect the rights of people

Disrespect to the rights of people is the cause of mob violence and this results in taking law by the people in their hands.

All of a sudden the country is witnessing a spate of violent incidents involving the common man, who has taken the law into his hands. Ten people, suspected to be thieves, were lynched in Vaishall district of Bihar. Within a week, two more were bludgeoned to death in the Sultanganj area of Patna. Five labourers were killed in Lonavala, Maharashtra, in a dispute over petty cash. In Kerala, a mob assaulted two women, one of them pregnant, for an alleged theft, prompting Prime Minister Manmohan Singh to express concern over repeated incidents of vigilantism at a national meeting of police chiefs.

These incidents show a lack of faith in the criminal justice system of the country. So, what drives people to beat, maim and kill others? Is it an inefficient police adminstration, a shoddy prosecution, or lethargic judiciary and prisons which allow dons to carry on their unlawful activities from within the safe confines, that make people lose confidence in the law of the land. The Malimath Committee on judicial reforms had warned us way back in 2004 that the criminal justice system was "virtually collapsing", that it was "slow, inefficient and ineffective", and, therefore, "people are losing confidence in the system". The Committee had made salutary recommendations, which unfortunately were trashed because of a cacophony of protests by vested interests, masquerading as human rights activists and champions of civil liberty. The much-needed reforms were shelved.

The Supreme Court gave specific directions on September 22, 2006, for comprehensive reforms in the functioning of the police. Many states have complied but the bigger ones are either being defiant or just pretending to be compliant. Gujarat has taken the stand that the directions would affect the federal character of the Constitution. Maharashtra has argued that the directions are against statutory provisions. It is a token compliance in Tamil Nadu and Uttar Pradesh while Bihar has passed an Act which is highly regressive. Unfortunately, there is every effort to delay, dilute and, if possible, sabotage the directions given by the apex court.

There is an all-round resistance to reforms. Politicians and bureaucrats want the status quo to continue as it ensures their hegemony over the different wings of the criminal justice administration. On the other hand, human rights activists can't think beyond the rights of criminals and terrorists.

No wonder, in an environment where society has to depend upon laws which were framed during colonial times and the process of reform is stalled by a myopic bureaucracy and a visionless political leadership, people who seek justice take recourse to desperate measures. The Naxalites have People's Courts, where ready but rough justice is dispensed. They revel in reducing a man's height by nine inches (in other words, beheading him). Similarly, others who have lost faith in the efficacy of the criminal justice administration administer their own sense of justice.

Mob rule

A mob by definition is born by the mutual raising of tension and comes together only to commit an act of violent protest. When it can be manipulated, it becomes dangerous and an uncontrollable blast. In a crowded, chaotic and conflict ridden country like India, mobs are born more frequently today because an already overloaded and over compromised judicial system continues to operate in an overheated climate watched by an over eager media audience. The domino effect of mob violence cannot be overestimated, especially as it is observed that perpetrators of public lawlessness are rarely identified or punished quickly. Such type of incidents reflect a general degradation in society and an impatience with the slow pace of the criminal justice system. Probably people these days want instant justice. Supreme Court Justice A.K. Mathur and Justice Katju have said, "people in the country are fast losing faith in the judiciary".

Rising rage

1. Delhi, Oct 7, 2007 - A mob goes on a rampage after a city bus kills seven.

2. Bengal Sept. 30, 2007 - Crowds attack ration shops at Labhpur in Birbhum District.

3. Bihar Sept. 13, 2007 - Ten people lynched in Dhulpurwa village Vaishali District.

4. U.P. Aug. 28, 2007 - A procession in Agra turns violent after truck kills four.

5. Hydrabad Oct.1, 2007 - Alleging that the principal of a convent school was misbehaving with girl students and forcing a school teacher to marry him, about 150 people ransacked the school and burnt the furniture.

6. Delhi Sept 22, 2007 - Two police posts were set on fire by a mob around Jamia Millia, Islamia university. About 40 people, including policemen, were injured in the course of an encroachment removal drive when the Koran was reportedly dropped by a policeman leading to violence.

7. Mumbai Nov. 30, 2006- Angered by the desecration of a B.R. Ambedkar Statue in Kanpur, Dalits in several parts of Maharastra went on rampage setting three trains on fire, damaging over 100 buses and clashing with the police in violent protests that left four dead and over 60 injured. Curfew was imposed in many areas.

8. Gurgaon July 25, 2005 - A protest by workers of Honda Motercycle and Scooter India factories seeking higher wages and

re-employment of suspended employee snowballed into a major confrontation in Gurgaon. Trouble started after the protestors attacked the police with stones and sticks near the ITI on the Mehrauli – Gurgaon road and torched the police vehicle, later the police surrounded the workers and thrashed them, leaving many with broken limbs.

9. Nagpur Aug. 13, 2004 - A criminal, Bharat alias, Akku Yadav involved in over two dozen cases of murder, extortion, dacoity, robbery, theft, rioting and molestation was brought to a court in Nagpur, when a mob comprising mostly of women, stormed the court room and lynched him. The court was not in session and the escorting constables had no option but to be a mute witness to the bizarre happening.

10. Kerala Oct. 7, 2007 - Two women were thrashed by a mob in Edappal on charge of theft. After 45 minutes, the women were rescued by a police team and found blameless. The state Human Rights Commission has suo-motu filed a case.

To say that mob violence and vigilantism have to do with the breakdown of law and order is, in a generic sense, pure truism. Naturally, if the law enforcement agencies are not effective, then incidents of not just vigilantism, but looting, burning and other kinds of violent crowd behaviour take over.

Yet, mob violence and vigilantism don't belong to the same category. There is, in fact, a fundamental difference behind the causes for these two species of lawlessness and violence. It is necessary to appreciate this difference if we want to tackle both mob violence and vigilantism. Vigilantism is when people, groups or individuals take law in their own hands and mete out exemplary punishment, for example, when prisoners eyes are gouged out, or when a suspected rapist is lynched. It needs to be noted that those who commit acts of this kind do it in full glare of the law, and indeed may even be policemen and lawyers, as the record in India shows. These demonstrations of vigilantism are not surreptitious, and are carried out with a good degree of public approval.

Mob violence, such as looting and torching of buses, is different These cases occur on the blind side of the law, and may happen any time, but surreptitiously vigilantism gets its specific flavour because it happens in routine circumstances and is like a conspiracy in the sun. Unlike mob behaviour, there is no obvious breakdown of law and order, and yet prisoners are made blind, a Scheduled Caste citizen is whipped in the premises of a court, and so on. In contrast, mob violence occurs when law enforcement officers lose their grip over a particularly tense situation. Buses are burnt, shops looted and people killed. The legal and constitutional systems are not threatened, but often find reinforcement after such wild acts of wanton destruction.

Vigilantism, which thrives on the breakdown of the legal machinery itself, has a different profile. In this sense, it is a greater threat to society. It thrives best in an atmosphere where there is an all-pervading cynicism towards the law. While mob riots are an outcome of an episodic breakdown of the law, for vigilantism there is no law but its own. Mob violence is socially less dangerous when compared to vigilantism.

A breakdown of the law can happen anywhere in the world, even in well-governed democratic societies. From Denmark to the UK and the USA, not to mention India, there have been instances of mob violence, usually controlled once the police or the paramilitary arrive on the scene.

Vigilantism thrives because of two factors. The first is the de-legitimation of the institution of law itself– the Penal Code, the Civil Code and even the Constitution. The second is that by acts of commission, and significant omission, those in power participate in breeding an atmosphere, conducive to vigilantism. Because political bosses found it useful, urban gangs nourished in the US from the 1930s right up to the time of World War I. Between the Wars, again, politicians used the Italian and Jewish mafia to serve their own ends. Only after World War II did the character of democratic governance in the US changed, leading to the demise of widespread gang activism. Therefore, if vigilantism is to take a dip, politicians at the top should show allegiance to the law.

Large parts of Africa are overcome by vigilante activism. This is understandable as the rulers of most of the countries in that continent skate on a thin legal surface. The widespread presence of this phenomenon has led scholars to take special interest in the study of vigilantism in Africa. Vigilantism has little to do with poverty. The American mobsters were not poor, and neither are the gang lords of Africa. Vigilanters are proud of their status and often occupy fairly powerful positions in society. They have the backing of the ruling classes when they are not the rulers themselves. In fact, vigilantism requires that the State machinery be corrupted from within. In contrast, those involved in mob violence are often frustrated and economically humiliated people. They feel dwarfed by the weight of their circumstances and hit out when nobody is looking.

So let us not give in to superficial explanations such as the breakdown of law and order or poverty and look at the broader structural features that encourage vigilantism. If vigilantism is growing in India, the fault lies in the upper reaches of our society and not at the base where the poor live. To equate vigilantism with mob violence is tantamount to covering up for the rich and the well-placed.

Vigilantism has been defined as "morally sanctimonious behaviour aimed at rectifying or remedying a structural flaw in society". The instances of mob violence which we are witnessing these days are a kind of protest against the structural flaws in our criminal justice system. In any case, vigilante activity is a threat to democracy and the Rule of Law.

It is not that other countries are immune to this phenomenon. In the US, vigilantism was witnessed in the eighteenth century when, in the absence of proper laws, certain voluntary associations got together to flog, torture, or even kill people who were perceived as threats to their communities. The trend reappeared, in what some experts call neo-vigilantism, in the 1920s and pseudo-vigilantism in the '70s. During the '20s when there was widespread disorder in China, the Big Sword Society protected life and property. In Philippines, the Davao Death Squad has been killing the city's alleged notorious criminals. In El Salvador, a group of retired police and military officers have taken upon themselves the duty of cleansing the country of "impure" social elements.

However, this is not to justify vigilantism, or people dispensing speedy justice of any kind. It was and remains a kind of wild justice bereft of a structured procedure, devoid of codified laws, where the accused hardly get an opportunity to defend themselves. The quantum of punishment is most often decided by a hysterical mob. There should be no place for such barbarian justice in any civilised society, much less in an emerging power, and a democracy, like India. The trend must be arrested or else it could lead to anarchic conditions. Police must perform its mandated role and for that the necessary structural changes must be carried out. A long-term remedy lies in revamping the criminal justice administration and enforcing the Rule of Law swiftly, within a time-frame and in an inexpensive manner.

People have lost faith in the criminal justice system. They feel that the rich and powerful will use clout, political power and money to exploit the loopholes in the system. Many also feel that the system does not function properly because it is lethargic and time consuming.

It is a basic human nature to retaliate, which is why a civilised justice system came into being. The idea behind establishing such a system was to counter man's basic instinct of revenge and instant justice and reassure him that the system will take care of the aggrieved and, with the evidence collected, will punish the accused. But when this does not happen, at the speed and in a manner that the victim wants, the natural instinct is back at play. Such a development does not bode well for society. This is what is currently happening in the country as more and more people try to seek justice.

There is also an increasing trend of savagery and people are becoming more violent and cruel, not hesitating to indulge in gruesome acts. Even in an affluent, civilised society, people resort to all kinds of violence either because of greed or because they want to satisfy their carnal urges. It is an "I don't care" attitude which seems to have become a global phenomenon. Just look at the shootings in the United States where a 20-year old policeman killed six teenagers in a remote Wisconsin state town called Crandon. The police shot dead the killer who had also killed his estranged girlfriend. Closer home, we have had a rash of incidents in which people have resorted to violence and taken the lives of others, including innocents. In Bangalore, a 32-year old hotel owner was murdered in a tiff over food. According to the police, 24-year old Srinivas Murthy went to a hotel and demanded food. As it was time to close, hotel owner Sudhir Kumar asked Murthy to leave which led to a quarrel. The next day Murthy, along with five accomplices, attacked Kumar with clubs and wooden sticks injuring him grievously. Kumar was rushed to the hospital where he succumbed to his injuries.

The entire criminal justice system needs to be revamped to make it more efficient and for that, it should be free of the control of our political leaders. One often hears these days of politicians' involvement in crime or their dependence on criminals. The system, therefore, has to be insulated from politicians. Investigations should also be handled by an independent professional body, with no political allegiance, in the same manner that judges are not accountable to political masters. Unfortunately, promotions and even transfers of investigating officers depend upon our political leaders who are liable to be biased.

Our investigating agencies have to be more efficient and professional and they should use modern, forensic and scientific methods. Investigations should be independent and autonomous. This is necessary as criminals today are intelligent, use sophisticated equipment and plan their acts meticulously. There is always competition between the law breaker and the law enforcer, where the enforcer generally is weak and less efficient which leaves the law breaker with the upper hand.

In early 2003, the Committee on Reforms of Criminal Justice System submitted its report to the government with comprehensive recommendations like making the quest for truth the guiding star of the entire criminal justice system and replacing proof beyond reasonable doubt in the Indian Evidence Act with clear and convincing standard of proof. Despite a big debate on the recommendations, not much has been implemented.

Ironically, violence in society is taking place at a time when there is an increased focus on human rights, equity and justice. The United Nations 1948 declaration of human rights was followed by many commissions on human rights which have created much awareness. Still there has been a phenomenal rise in crime, even rise in cruelty. Criminals have become brutish and are willing to go to any length to commit a crime and against anyone. Even crime against children has gone up. Earlier, religion and moral values used to play a significant role in containing these animal instincts. Now, it seems even our existing laws, which should act as a deterrent, have failed to stop criminals.

Maybe it is time that we look at bringing in a higher moral law to regulate our inner workings. A strong moral fibre may be successful in regulating our lives as the existing legal and administrative system is not being properly followed. We need to look within and see how we can police ourselves instead of putting in all our energies into the existing criminal justice system.

The Vaishali Lynchings

As per report in *India Today* of Oct. 2007: In the face of police inaction, villagers of Dhelpurwa village in Bihar's Vaishali district brutally killed 10 men suspected of being thieves. Two of those involved now tell their story.

Ranjit Kureri, 20 the lone survivor of the Vaishali lynching that left 10 dead:

"It was almost 4 in the morning when we reached Dhelpurwa on our way to Tajpur Banjara village after attending a party. It was a long trek and some of us had drunk a lot of country liquor. We had no money but wanted a ride. We woke a three-wheeler driver but he turned abusive, after which one of us slapped him hard. The driver started shouting which attracted the villagers. They were angry and wanted to know who we were. Despite our best efforts, we failed to convince them. In a couple of minutes a few young villagers started hecking and shoving us. We were frightened and some of us tried to escape. The villagers caught us and started beating us with whatever they could lay their hands on; stones, bricks and sticks. Our cries seemed to only provoke them more as they continued beating us for what must have been almost two hours. I escaped because I pretended to be dead. The police found me and took me to a hospital. It was later that I learnt we were suspected of being thieves and 10 of my companions have been beaten to death."

A burly man in his forties, who admits to being one of the Dhelpurwa attackers.

"There had been thefts in the village for the past six months. There were three burglaries in a fortnight, yet the police took no action, and so we started patrolling the village on our own. Initially, walking under the night sky was fun but soon enough, we grew irritable. Who likes to miss a good night's sleep? All we desperately wanted was to catch a thief and when we caught a pack of them, we meted out justice then and there. We never meant to kill them. We were only interrogating them, slapping them lightly, when some tried to escape. So we caught them and beat them with bricks and bamboos till they died. The police never paid any attention to our complaints so we have no remorse when we took the law into our hands. It was not planned. Nobody instigated us. We were just angry and frustrated. There seemed no other option. Although we are not inhuman, I must admit, some of us actually enjoyed the lynching. At least we got rid of these criminals. Our only regret is that one thief survived and another escaped".

Control of mob

Following are the tested measures to control the mob:

1. Mobs tend to adopt hit and run tactics. They disappear when chased but gather again after a time when the police have moved to another trouble spot. Such guerrilla type tactics continue unabated, giving the impression that the police are not doing anything to control the riots. Actually, the police are led a merry dance on such occasions because they are heavily outnumbered. Their opponents reappear like jacks-inboxes at regular intervals at the most unexpected places. Mobs are composed of mostly ordinary people who would not normally indulge in violence. They are encouraged to do so by the fact that they constitute only one of a great multitude of men like themselves, who feel that the chance of getting caught is very slim. Anonymity is what gives them courage.

Members of a mob have a collective personality which is quite different from the individual personalities of the people forming the mob. The police officer entrusted with controlling a mob has to find a way of splintering this collective personality so that each individual in the mob is made to think as an individual.

2. No policemen will act in riot situations without being led. It is not that they sympathize with the rioters, but they are not prepared to take any responsibility or risk. If an officer, particularly a senior one, gives an order, they will comply.
3. The policemen, once they get into action, do not know when to stop. They wield their lathis with gay abandon, even on young boys trying to escape from the spot. They also unnecessarily belabour men who have fallen during the stampede. Sometimes, three or more policemen concentrate on one fallen rioter though they could have chased others.
4. The deployment of police reserves and reinforcements, called from outside the district or city, is more often than not very haphazardly done. The main squares of the affected city or town are immediately guarded by police pickets, whereas the rioters choose the numerous lanes and *galis* to taunt and harass the order-keeping forces. If the reinforcements are ordered to move to one of the affected streets, very soon the officer on the spot is compelled to move his troops to a neighbouring street or *gali* to meet the exigencies of a developing situation. The end result is to invite the criticism that the police were nowhere to be seen at the trouble spots when what actually happens is that the trouble spots themselves proliferate and change very frequently during the course of the day.
5. Sending an arrested man or even a few such men to the police stations at such times seriously depletes your man-

power. You have to depute two men at least, with a lone culprit. If there are ten culprits arrested, then at least half a dozen men would be required to prevent them from disappearing. This, in turn, reduces the effective strength required for essential operations. It would also involve sending a vehicle which is badly required for the operations. The men sent would return in their own sweet time, some of which would be spent in the paper work that is so much a part of all police procedures. It is for this reason that most officers avoid making spot arrests. If they do so, they keep the accused seated in police vans with a couple of armed men to guard them. At the end of the day, they are transported to the police stations for further legal action.

The use of any force at all depends on the mood of the mob and the personality of the senior most police officer in-charge at the spot. His ability to communicate with the mob and force the members of the mob to think as individuals is extremely important. A mob has a collective personality, different from the individuals who constitute it. This collective personality is very aggressive though individuals constituting the mob may themselves be sober and docile. The expertise of the police officer lies in splintering the collective personality of the mob. Very often this may require the most extreme of measures such as the use of firearms.

The use of firearms has been routinely criticized by human rights and other concerned groups, particularly in the western countries where riotous mobs are not a common phenomenon, as they are in India. Not being accustomed to such street violence, they cannot understand why unarmed protesters should be shot at. They are unable to appreciate that when a mob takes to looting and burning, its numbers soon increase because lumpen elements take advantage of the situation to burn and loot. The respect for law, which is second nature to people in the West, is not a feature of our existence. Force has to be used on many occasions, and unfortunately, some deaths do result as a consequence of the force used by the police. Without the use of force, when it is inevitable, the loss to life and property would be far greater.

There is a misconception in the public mind that the police has first to make a lathi charge, after which tear gas is discharged; and only after these two exercises have failed can the police turn to their firearms. Ideally, it is the duty and responsibility of the police to prevent deaths and destruction. If a mob is on the rampage and it is not possible to go through the drill of warning the rioters, making lathi charges, and discharging tear gas, bullets may have to be fired to prevent further damage to life and property. The man at the spot has to decide the nature of the force required to be employed. He does not have much time to make up his mind.

Very often mob violence can be controlled without the use of force. One could try humour or do something particularly funny or ridiculous to distract the attention of the people constituting the mob. More often than not, however, force has to be used to disperse the rioters. In such cases, the force should be of the type or of the magnitude that makes them think as individuals. Individuals should be given ample scope to escape and run as far away as possible so that they do not regroup again with a new group of 'friends'. Unfortunately, in a country as large as ours, with so many people, often led by anti-social elements it becomes necessary to shoot a few rounds at the rioters to compel them to disperse specially when they are killing, burning and looting with murderous intent and are out of the range of lathis. At such times, only the use of tear gas shells or bullets can stop the mayhem and prevent greater loss to life and property. A determined mob may not be deterred by tear gas. It is usual for the rioters to cover their eyes, nose and mouth with wet cloth and kick away the tear gas shells back to the police. It the mob loses the fear of authority, the result is an escalation of the rioting and greater destruction of life and property. It has to be remembered that people do not forgive the police if they use less lethal methods of dispersal when the occasion so demands. The use of firearms by the police should be strictly under the control and direction of the magistrates or their own senior officers.

In the aftermath of such riots maintaining pickets in the places where riots had erupted, arranging for their regular relief and supervision, and finally starting investigations into the numerous cases of rioting, arson and looting that had been registered is indeed a big problem. Special teams of officers should be formed for this purpose in each of the city police stations, and this keeps the designated officers busy. It is not easy to gather evidence to link the arrested rioters with specific cases of looting or arson. It is easier to prosecute the receivers of the loot, if and when they had stored them in their own houses. Receivers of stolen property are as criminal-minded as thieves. The difficulty arises because the Courts demand absolute proof that that particular piece of property was in fact stolen.

Every police officer and every ordinary policeman tries to throw his weight about and use the powers given to him to establish his own superiority over the common mortals. They do not pause to think that a position of authority and the powers reposed in them is a trust to be used for the benefit of the people they serve. If they use it wisely in a spirit of justice and humanity, the returns will be far greater. It is a pity that the young officers of today do not find time to mingle with their own men. If they do have some leisure time, they follow their own individual pursuits and pay scant attention to this very important aspect of human relations. The fact that the officers have lost touch with their men has adversely affected discipline in the police forces. The common excuses are that they are extremely busy with law and order duties and VIP bandobast. The problem is that the importance of human relations, so essential in a uniformed force, is not only neglected but totally ignored by most officers. Efficiency and success rates will definitely improve if the seniors try to reverse this trend.

(h) POLITICS IN TERRORISM

Let us try to understand the politics involved in terrorism.

Why do we need to change the contours of the anti-terror discourse? Because saffron too has surfaced in a jehadi mode? A cursory look at the backdrop might help. In a 1,000 years of living together in harmony, enriching each others music, art architecture – the list is inexhaustible – of course we differed, and clashed. But it was our quarrel and we settled it. Becoming a link in the global war on terror, outsideres will have fingers on our levers. This is dangerous. Riots in the past had simple origins. Muslim boy runs away with Hindu girl or the other way around. The passage of one's religious procession through the "sensitive" localities of the other. And, of course, cow slaughter. Pig's meat found in a mosque. Terrorism entered our discourse only after 9/11. US bombardment of Afghanistan dominated 24x7 global and national channels. In the midst of this saturation coverage of the "war on terror" the December 13, 2001 attack on Indian Parliament resulted in heightened Indo-Pak tension, causing fears of a nuclear exchange . It was in this state of stoked up anti-terror hysteria that leaders made rabble rousing anti-SIMI speeches in Kanpur on the eve of the Februrary 2002 UP assembly elections.The political party choreography was straight forward in the charged "anti-terrorist" atmosphere. Wild celebrations in Ayodhya would be "controlled" by the "Party of governance" and they would go from strength to strength. In the event, something dramatically different happened. On February 25, 2002 the Karsevaks, assembled in Ayodhya for victory celebrations, were dejected and angry. In fierce anger, they crowded into the Ahmedabad- bound Sabarmati Express, on the way to Godhra. Followed by the Februrary 2002 Gujarat Pogrom, Godhra is the first terrorist incident in Indian history leading to an unprecedented pogrom which created the atmosphere in which Narendra Modi won. The sequence of events, political currents and caste sociology of Gujarat have not been properly studied.

It is universally acknowledged that heightened tensions with Pakistan, militancy in Kashmir and Indian Muslims brought into focus on 24x7 in the terrorism frame, help polarise people and votes. The process alienates minorities, but it helps in "Hindu consolidation". There were political uses of "terror". The neo-con directed war on terror and its amplification on the global media coalesed with the Indian media's obsessive incantation of the terror mantra. This may have been for TRP ratings but it served the ends of "Hindu" politics. Conspiracy theorists talked of two unspoken agendas that were being pursued. One was an arcane pursuit of an international triangle: Washington-Jerusalem-New Delhi. The theory was that Jews and the Hindus were both surrounded by hostile Muslims and Muslim states, and that both will have security joining hands with each other and with an ever powerful US. The global war on terror would have this outcome as one of its consequences. The other theory focused on terrorism to alienate minorities and work towards "Hindu consolidation" to obviate caste and tribal division. But India has the world's second largest Muslim population and not an insubstantial number of Christians. To fight terror is essential. But to develop a political interest in the atmosphere created by terror is lethal. Of course, there are misguided hot heads on both sides of the religious divide. The purpose of the recent terror plot was tit-for-tat, but it had another more diabolical purpose: it was to keep up the atmospherics of terror which, in the ultimate, is associated in popular consciousness with "Muslims" and "Jihad". The principal aim was to amply the atmospherics generated by terror that is conducive to divisive politics. Hindu terror. It's a term that a certain section of the media and politicians simply love. And they have been vigorously cuddling it for long. It's a great stick to beat their so-called non-secular opponents. Some stray, unsubstantiated allegations about the involvement of Hindu minded persons in a number of recent bomb blasts has helped this section to jubilantly claim that terrorism is not a 'Muslim only' phenomenon but has an equally sinister Hindu angle to it. Buoyed by the kind of high-profile media backing selective leaks by the Maharashtra ATS has received, the organisation has now gone ballistic. Short of charging "Hindu terrorists" of being responsible for 9/11, the blame for virtually every terror incident is being slapped on the Hindutva forces.

Let's examine the media reports clinically. First, despite a succession of narco-tests on alleged Hindu terorists, no significant leads have yet been found. The failure to ferret out incriminating details has been atributed to a Hindu Sadhvi's training in the art of meditation, (which apparently strengthens the intellect to resist entrapment efforts even in a drugged state) or an army officer's ability to withstand cross-questioning despite being plied with narcotic substances. Second, all we have been told are some purported confessions of Lt. Col Shrikant Purohit, which are not only self-contradictory but also fly in the face of previous assertions by official investigating agencies, especially in the matter of the Samjhauta Express blasts. On the basis of such untenable allegations stands the edifice of "Hindu terror". The preposterous, state-sponsored conspiracy to equate "Hindu terror" with Jihadi terror falters hopelessly because the whole world has been subject to rampant terrorism by organisations owing allegiance to the Al-Qaeda or its variants – from New York to London and Madrid, Afghanistan, Iraq, Indonesia, Pakistan, India, China and even Kenya. It can be nobody's case that there should be positive discrimination in favour of terrorists sporting non-Islamic badges. But to suggest that the alleged actions of one motorcycle-borne Sadhvi, self-styled Swami, a few political activists, one serving and a few retired Indian army personnel constitutes "Hindu terror" amounts to demanding a permanent willing suspension of disbelief. Are those who question the ATS's daily litany of fresh accusations against the randomly arrested group guilty of double standards? It is often alleged that if one accepts the security forces' charges against SIMI and its cohorts, one should be equally ready to swallow the ATS's line on Pragya, Purohit, et al. However, there is a huge difference between the two cases. Many SIMI and other Jihadi terror mongers have already been brought to book and being tried in courts. The most celebrated of the lot, Afzal Guru, has been found guilty by the Supreme Court and sentenced to death. That the incumbent dispensation in New Delhi does not have the guts to execute the order for fear of antagonising its vote-bank is another matter. But this distinction between the two cases. Let the courts pronounce the "Hindu terrorist" guilty and, if so, let the verdicts be executed. But they cannot be pilloried on the basis of specious confessions, which could well be figments of a beleaguered ATS's shaky imagination. Even if for a moment we accept that some Hindus have indulged in copycat acts, it must be borne in mind that the majority of Indians are shocked, outraged, angry and even vengeful because of relentless terrorist depredations. Nearly 10,000 innocent people have died at the hands of bloodthirsty jihadi terrorists over the past 15 years. If some people, howsoever misguided, attempt to avenge this because the state fails to provide security or succour is quite natural. This is not to justify the vigilante action, but only try and explain it. If the state does not shed its hypocrisy the alleged Malegaon plot may only be the beginning. Terrorism is a response by alienated groups to express their anger and resentment against a system, which they preceive has denied them justice and equal treatment. Terrorist violence, then, aims to create intense anxiety and a sense of insecurity among citizens as well as destabilise the political system. Terrorism then cannot have a single colour, whether from the end of the perpetrator or the victims. People of one colour are not targeted. Those who die cut across communities and colour. Nor do the perpetrators of terrorist violence have a single colour. Alienation from the system is not an attribute of a particular sections of society. It can arise in any religious or cultural tradition. There is common belief that some religious traditions contain elements, which render their followers particularly prone to militancy and terrorism. What is often ignored is that there are in all religious tradition both aggressive and pacifist elements, under what specific historical conditions a particular religion throws up aggressive or militant responses has to be seen against the context in which such responses arise. History bears witness that all world religion, including Hinduism, have at some point or the other thrown up terrorist responses. If there has been Jewish, Christian or Islamic Terrorism, why should we assume that there cannot be Hindu terrorism? From this perspective, it would be naive to believe that Hinduism is incapable to throwing up militant responses though such strange claims have been advanced by the leaders of Hindutva. Since the early days of the rise of nationalism, a section of the Hindus, represented by the Hindu Mahasabha and the RSS advocated militant line. The problem in the case of Hindutva militancy is complicated: Hindutva is committed to fascism and creation of a Hindu Rashtra where the 'other' would either not exist or would occupy the status of second-class citizens.

The hue and cry that ensued the Batla House encounter in Okhla area, New Delhi and the widespread arrest of educated Muslim youths in Azamgarh and other towns, in which liberal Muslim sections also vociferously joined in, was prompted by the growing perception that the law enforement agencies had become highly communalised and were deliberately targeting Muslim educated youth. It is possible that this reaction was an exaggerated response, but it is undeniable that the security thinking in recent years is that the minorities represent a security threat and should be guarded against. Statements from leaders that a distinction had to be drawn between nationalism and communalism, implying that Hindu communalism is necessarily nationalist whereas minority communalism is inherently anti-national, consolidated such perceptions. This obviously represents a systemic failure on the part of the state. The constitutional and political edifice of this country was raised on the premise that every one who lives in it is an equal citizen and enjoys the same rights and protection. This vision, enshrined in the constitution, is increasingly becoming a dead letter. Operating on the premise that the people of India were extremely religious and if a proactive line of secularisation of society was pursued there would be strong public reaction, the state want on making compromises.

One consequence of this has been that over the years religious consciousness has grown manifold and middle class, which is crucial to shaping public perceptions, itself has become increasingly communalised. So, it is to be expected that faith in the state would be undermined and people would only unwillingly believe the impartiality of the state and its institutions. There is need to recognise that the vision of India promising equality, social justice and fair treatment to its citizens, of whatever hues, has to be restored. So long as that does not happen, we are likely to be caught up in the quagmire of terrorism and frequent meaningless controversies.

Tough action is required

Terrorism seems to have taken the entire country in its grip. There is hardly a state which is not affected by the terrorist menace, though the shades may be different. There is 'ethnic terror' in the north-east, 'Naxalite terror' over vast swathes of central India and there is the 'Islamist terror' which, starting from J&K, has spread to other parts of the country. Of these, the last one is undoubtedly the most devastating by virtue of its linkages with the forces of global jihad. Their objectives may be different — separatism for the north-eastern rebels, new democratic revolution for the Naxals, and azadi for the militants in J&K. But in practical terms, these boil down to creating communal disharmony, disrupting the economy and destabilsing the political structure. A grim scenario is building up which calls for comprehensive strategy. The salient features of the terrorist threat need to be clearly understood. First, it has today an all-India sweep, from Kashmir to Kanyakumari and Mumbai to Guwahati. Second, the terrorists, with their sophisticated weaponry and expertise in the use of IEDs, pack an enormous punch. Third, the frequency of these attacks is now anybody's guess. Earlier, it was one major incident every quarter. Now another incident could happen tomorrow or just any other day. Fourth, while the Naxalite movement is more or less entirely indigenous, the north-eastern insurgents and the Islamist terrorists have a significant nexus with external forces which enable them to get weapons, ammunition and explosives from our neighbouring countries, apart from access to sanctuaries, training facilities and guidance. Yes, we should show the political will, chalk out a comprehensive plan and extend necessary legal and administrative support to the states irrespective of the governing party to effectively face the terror. There are three outstanding examples of our success against terrorism. Punjab offers the best illustration. The state witnessed what was one of the most lethal terrorist movements the world has seen, and yet it was vanquished. In Andhra Pradesh, which had become the epicentre of Naxal movement in the country, the state police have been able to clear the affected districts of the Maoists, who have since fled to the neighbouring states. In Tripura the security forces have been able to break the bone of the ATTF and the NLFT, the major insurgent groups operating in the state. There is no reason why the central and the state governments, working in tandem, cannot contain the terrorist threat we face today. We should, to start with, define our anti-terror policy in unambiguous terms, and make it clear that the country shall not compromise in its battle with terrorism under any circumstances; that it shall be dealt with sternly and at all costs. At the same time, the state must give an assurance that legitimate political demands will be met and that genuine socio-economic grievances shall be addressed. This policy will have to be backed by appropriate structural changes in the law enforcement machinery. A federal investigating agency must be set up in view of the fact that terrorist crimes have interstate or even international ramifications. The state police agencies, with their compartmentalised approach, would not be able to do justice to such cases.

The state police units, it must be remembered, are our first line of defence against terrorism. These must be energised and motivated. The police stations should be strengthened and the system of beat patrol revived. Unfortunately, we have allowed the state satraps to politicise these forces and blunt their striking power. In a couple of states, the ruling parties are using them virtually as their private militias. The Supreme Court directions on police reforms should be implemented without any further delay. The apex court itself would have to crack the whip against the recalcitrant states. The investigation and law and order work must be separated in the metropolitan towns at least. Intelligence must be insulated from political influences and revamped on the lines recommended by the Saxena committee. There is a Money Laundering Act on the statute book but it needs to be made more stringent because the terrorist outfits continue to indulge in hawala transactions in a significant way. The UN Security Council Resolution 1373 lays great stress on choking the financial sources of terrorists.

A stringent anti-terror law is a must. The argument that the existence of TADA or POTA in the past did not finish terrorism is juvenile. Notwithstanding the existence of the Indian Penal Code, we still have incidents of murder and rape. Does it mean that the penal sections relating to these crimes could be abolished? Besides, if a particular law is misused, the answer lies in incorporating safeguards and ensuring that those overstepping the limits of law are suitably punished. Throwing the baby out with the bathwater is no solution.

We are a nuclear power. We aspire to have a permanent seat in the UN Security Council. But we are looking pathetic and clueless in the face of recurring terrorist attacks in our cities. including the national capital. A determined and firm response is called for. Veerbhogya Vasundhara (the brave shall rule the earth). say our ancient texts. The terrorist threat can surely be contained, if not demolished, once we decide that national security shall take precedence over all other considerations.

Dealing with Terror

The toll of 180 human lives is heavy but the psychological impact has been far greater on India and its people, as also on those from abroad. There has been an intensity of public outrage and international solidarity not seen before, which has long-term implications. While attack was on, one missed leadership of the calibre of Rudi Giulani, New Yorks dynamic mayor at the time of 9/11. Political leadership seemed remote, and sometimes callous, and this elicited a sharp response from the public. At the same time, the security forces and fire servicemen were deservedly praised for their courage and determination in facing the situation, despite many handicaps. The Muslim community, in particular, must be lauded for their forthright and strong denunciation of the attack in Mumbai and expressions of solidarity with India's core values. In the wake of this terrible episode, the Government and the people are responding with vigour and energy. The major responses are the formation of a National Investigation Agency (NIA) for intelligence-related counter-terrorism, a Coastal Command for stronger maritime security, and a specific anti-terrorism Law. There are numerous problems and pitfalls on the road to all three, which can only be avoided by a far-sighted political leadership and the constructive and sincere co-operation of all entities involved, be it the State governments, or the security and intelligence agencies. The people must monitor this process closely and not allow any slackening of effort or descent into petty turf wars. For too long, the country has suffered from violent insurgencies, and armed extremists of every shade and political persuasion, who see the gun as a short-cut to their political ends. Terrorism has strong links with crimes such as smuggling, extortion, and human trafficking. Organised crime, which has burgeoned in India due to a cosy relationship with some elements of the political class and law enforcement agencies, provides a source of support and logistics for terrorists, and a nexus develops between them. It is essential that all the entities concerned are involved in the setting up of the counter-terrorism agency and the coastal command. It is time, therefore, to crack down on organized crime as well. It is a pity that Dawood remains a threat to India even if he is outside the country. Is there really no way to suppress his Indian operations and why have they grown so monstrously? What are the vested interests that prevent this? Much has been said about the "root causes" of terrorism. Dr Vamik Volkan, an expert on the psychology of terrorism has some interesting insights. His thesis is that persons whose lives are disrupted by social or political upheavals or conflicts have traumas inflicted upon their sense of personal identity, which is normally supported by several layers of membership, such as the family, clan, village or local community, social and religious groups, country, etc. Disruptions affecting any of these can cause traumas and alienation from mainstream society and feelings of low self-esteem. Such persons then become target for conversion to terror as part of a deliberate exploitation plan that implants a large group identity into him while injecting selectively religious justification for killing so-called enemies. It follows, therefore, that society must provide effective means for such "disrupted identity" persons to rejoin the mainstream society in an inclusive and constructive manner. India's ethos of multicultural understanding provides a sound foundation for building strong social cohesion. A further problem is that the longer terrorism persists, the more difficult it becomes to wean away terrorists, especially the young, to normal peaceful lives. This has been the experience in situations such as Lebanon and Angola, for example. In our region, terrorism has various faces — some internal, some external. Externally inspired terrorism has come from all sides of India. Our neighbours have different circumstances which give rise to terrorist threats to us. The recent Mumbai episode should be seen as part of a series of attacks that will probably continue into the future, as terrorists develop their skills and equipment.

Dealing with Threat

We desperately need a strong counter-terrorism system in place, sharpened by repeated drills and exercises, with full civil society participation, in order to deal with these very real threats.

Conventional criminal justice systems were never designed to deal with terrorism or even organised crime. At the most they may be able to sentence the apprehended and convicted perpetrators, who are merely expendable foot-soldiers. The battle against terror is more like a war against an enemy force, and we need to decapitate its generals and commanders, deprive it of resources and mobility, and destroy its communications, command and control. This calls for covert operations across borders in case the host country is unable or unwilling to take strong measures. But for successful covert operations such as those carried out by Israel, highest quality intelligence, commitment, preparations and political support are needed. How do we ensure high quality intelligence and analysis? There should be no misuse of intelligence capability by targeting political rivals. The target should be only terrorist entities and their front organizations. A high degree of professionalism and co-ordination, and information exchange amongst various agencies — civil, military, and technical, is called for. Creating the NIA may not by itself solve the underlying problem of lack of co-operation and co-ordination among existing entities with expertise and capability. It should be empowered to harness all the capabilities of the IB, RAW, military intelligence agencies, and State governments to deal with terrorism. In organisational reform, creating new boxes or entities does not work if the basic problems of attitude and commitment are not resolved. The proposed Coastal Command is an opportunity for a thorough review of the security responsibility for the coasts zones, from 0 to 200 km, where different agencies now have responsibilities. The Coast Guard must be made stronger, and the crack-down on smuggling intensified even if it causes some pain to vested interests. There has been much discussion of the fact that public order is a State subject under the 7th Schedule of our Constitution. In 1952, nobody foresaw the rise of terrorism. Be that as it may nothing prevent the Central Government from signing agreements or MoUs with each State Government under which counter terrorism could be dealt with by the Centre. To win the battle, it is essential for the Central and State governments to work together, putting aside narrow political considerations. The proposed law on terrorism has been a source of considerable contention. The human rights aspects, the due process of law and the need for deterrent punishment of terrorists need to be reconciled. Much care and much consultation with all affected parties is needed while drafting a good anti-terrorism law, and the best practices in this regard followed by other countries should be examined. All these challenges will be faced and overcome with the support of, and persistent pressure from, the people of India, awakened by the recent terrible experience.

Mumbai Attack on 26/11

Our post-Mumbai attack of 26/11 strategy has not been upto the mark and lacked purposefulness and coherence. Though Indian diplomatic offensive to mount pressure on Pak, along with solid evidence of LeT hand, has paid off as they have registered a FIR and six culprits have been arrested. Bowing down to the international pressure and based on the evidence supplied by the Indian Govt they have taken action. But by dilly-dallying tactics knowingly or unknowingly the Pak Govt has facilitated the group involved in Mumbai attack to destroy the evidences which could have been gathered by their prompt and immediate action in the case. Pakistan is repeatedly harping on purchase of five SIM cards in India which have been used by the terrorists in Mumbai. However the Indian counterpart has already clarified in the matter that those SIMs had been purchased in India but taken to Pakistan via Bangladesh.

World is closely watching terrorism born on Pak soil. The US in particular has renewed focus on Afganistan and Pakistan under Obama administration. They have withheld $5.5m aid to Pakistan demanding more accountability in war against terror. It appears we have been too cautious to the extent that it may salvage the policy of engagement with Pakistan pursued in recent years. We have been defensive in accusing elements in Pakistan and not the State Agencies despite the common belief that such a highly organized skillful commando operation could not have been possible without institutional support and connivance. We already have evidence against ISI involvement in blasting our Kabul Embassy. It appeared as if victim India has been reduced to petitioning for justice from guilty Pakistan. There should be clear cut distinction between crime and terror. The dimension of terrorism has to be dealt with a firm hand. We calculated that the Pakistan State may collapse and the country's nuclear power may fall into the hands of extremist elements, will ultimately overcome any real pressure on the country.

Takeaways from the Mumbai attacks

What are the key takeaways for the authorities and civilians from the way Mumbai handled the recent terror attack crisis?

"We tend to think of terrorist incidents, as mass bombings, etc. However, in reality, terrorist's use of firearms is very prevalent worldwide," says Mr. Raymond E. Foster, a retired Lieutenant of the Los Angeles Police Department, author and college lecturer. He is also, as Wikipedia mentions, one of the leading authorities in law enforcement technology, police research, and counterterrorism strategies. He is the editor of *Hi Tech Criminal Justice Newsletter* (www.hitechcj.com)

Mr. Foster suggests, during the course of a recent email interaction with *Business Line*, a simple exercise to prove his point about firearms: "Query the Lawson Terrorism Information Centre database, with information going back many years, you will find thousands of terrorism-related incidents wherein a firearm was the primary method of attack." Terrorists and criminals with firearms differ in one major way. Criminals use the guns as means of committing crime and facilitating escape, whereas terrorists use them to inflict casualties. This means that the terrorists are going to keep shooting until they exhaust their ammunition and/or they are incapacitated by first responders.

This places a huge burden on first responders. First responders must be equipped at least as well as the terrorists. We learned this hard way in Los Angeles, but now equip at least one police car in each geographic area with a high-power semi-automatic weapon. Additionally, first responders must be trained to respond to these incidents. Since the shooters (terrorists) are going to keep shooting until stopped, first responders must be trained to move towards and engage; this is dangerous and counter to the long-standing police procedure which used to be surround, contain and negotiate. While the first responders should at least be able to adequately defend themselves and preliminarily engage the shooters, domestic law enforcement and security must have, at reasonable rapid recall, highly trained counter-forces. In the US, this is accomplished with *SWAT,* Tactical Teams and Emergency Response Teams. This means that very well trained and highly equipped personnel can be committed to the incident within a 60-90 minute timeframe. A caveat to all of the first responder and follow-on activity by law enforcement is the Mumbai incident which is similar to the Beslan School siege in that it points out that terrorist organisations have different echelons of training and personnel. A suicide bomber is not likely a well-trained asset, on the other hand, a team of gunmen is very likely well-trained, equipped and mission orientated. This means domestic law enforcement and security are likely in the future to face small squads of terrorists employing military small-unit tactics ambushes.

Mumbai and Terror

Even for a country distressingly familiar with terrorist outages, the multiple attacks in Mumbai herald a new low. The sheer audacity and scale of the attacks, the spectacle of young men armed to the teeth with machine guns and grenades roaming on the streets of India's financial capital, bring home the fact that terrorism has attained a new sophistication and organizational ability. To talk of an intelligence failure is almost a truism, yet given that such a large group of men could physically launch attacks on multiple high-profile targets, eschewing the recent pattern of engineering blasts, is clear of an abysmal deficiency in our intelligence gathering capabilities. To combat such a new level of terrorism, it is imperative the contours of the extant anti-terror paradigm change. Terror has simply been politicized, with parties using it as yet another electoral plank. The scale of this latest outrage demonstrates the pitfalls of a divisive polity squabbling over instrumentalities. The need of the hour, and the future, is for political parties to break with past patterns and evolve a clear consensus on how to prevent the recurrence of such heinous attacks. To ensure a better security culture, and the involvement of every citizen in contributing to it, is also a matter of shaping a thoroughly neutral investigative apparatus. The issue of abysmal intelligence gathering also has to do with the perception of investigative agencies as being partisan. This has also led to severing of links between effect policing and intelligence gathering and various communities and groups. The Prime Minister has in the past spoken on the need for wider police reforms, and we could not agree more. The wider aspect of such reform, however, should also be to address the rifts within civil society. The spectacle of young men engaged in such brutally invasive terrorist acts, with no thought whatsoever as to concealing their identities also posits that idea of a collapsed civil society. And beyond measures such as preparedness and response, the extremism that feeds such fanatical acts needs to be addressed in the wider socio-political arena. That is, without doubt, and as various nations around the world have discovered, the best kind of pre-emptive measure.

That said, installing effective anti-terror mechanisms are also a matter of intra-state and international cooperation. While domestic measures such as institutionalizing state coordination among investigative agencies would be imperative, India should now press hard for greater intelligence sharing within the region. These attacks have also demonstrated a new level in the terrorists capabilities. The organizational and logistical abilities they have displayed are staggering. Both in the kind of targets chosen, the scale of the destruction and bloodbath, as well as the fact that for the first time, western nationals were sought to be targeted for greater international impact, point to a sharp escalation in terrorist ambitions. And even the response and management capabilities of the state have been shown to be glaringly low. That such an immense attack, almost akin to a mini-invasion, should have happened in Mumbai, home to one of the most respected police forces in India only underlines that fact. Another aspect of terrorism relates to how security forces are able to respond in a situation where hostages are taken by terrorists. The National Security Guards (NSG), where commandos are drawn from the army, has the wherewithal to do so. But the NSG has limited numbers and is a national level organization. The NSG is trained specifically for such situations. It would be a good idea to create state-level NSG-like modules, which are ready to act swiftly when such incidents occur.

Random Terror

Most of us can understand that terror strikes are unpredictable. But what one fails to understand is the predictable ham-handed response that we as nation seem to adopt when dealing with terrorist attacks. More so, given that India is now the most favoured destination when it comes to terrorist attacks. What has transpired in Mumbai, in those two days, is probably the wrost terrorist strike ever, save the sequence of events that transpired in New York on September 11, 2001.

For Mumbai this is the déjà vu. Over the past few years no other city in the world has suffered more at the hands of terrorists. The only thing more frightening than the regularity with which these strikes take place is the impunity with which these are carried out and the ineptness with which we deal with a terrorist situation. One would have thought that with every successive experience our ability to deal with a terrorist situation would improve. The truth though is that the state has failed to put together any sort of credible mechanism, either at the policy level or at the ground level, to deal with a terrorist situation and responses are at best ad hoc. They are daringly different from the ones the country has witnessed so far. Till now the attacks had been clandestine with the terrorists taking extreme precautions to cover their identity. Terrorism is a national problem and it is time not to hide behind the letter of the Constitution and treat it like a state subject.

The NSG, which is the elite force to deal with such situations, is centralized and located only in Delhi. Could more lives have been saved in Mumbai if we had the good sense to ensure that there are NSG units in all major cities? There is also no mechanism which ensures that all relevant intelligence relating to terror will be shared between various states. After every terror attack, intelligence agency of some states or the other will claim that it had warned the victim of the possibility of an attack and the warning was ignored. Rather than collaboration, all that one witnesses is competitiveness and one-upsmanship often based on political rivalry. However, it is the police who have suffered the most on account of archaic policy. Scores of terrorist attacks on and with hundreds of policemen dead or wounded, nobody gives the structural problems of the police force a thought. While the terrorists seem to have state-of-the art weapons, most of our policemen are still armed with only a stick. Even the few who are armed seem to largely possess dated weaponry. Most of them are sent to a terrorist scene with little or no armour and when such armour is provided it seems woefully inadequate. The helmet and the vest that the head of the ATS squad was donning minutes before his death, as seen on national T.V. never seemed to inspire any confidence. Neither did the image a few months back of a bomb disposal squad officer defusing a bomb without so much as a fire resistant suit. Policeman's life is just as important as those that he is trying to save and it is the duty of the state to do all it can to ensure this. If we can blow hundreds of crores sending an unmanned vehicle to the moon then surely we can afford to buy the best equipment available in the world for our police force. Despite so many incidents of terror, there is still no attempt to create an elite force of cops which can deal with terror situations.

At the ground level things are even worse. Take for example the Bombay VT station, which was one of the places attacked. Only a few months ago there was much ado about the installing of what are supposedly bomb detectors. There were numerous points where you could enter the station without ever passing through any of these detectors. Security checks at hotels, malls and office buildings often mean that every car will have a mirror shoved below the undercarriage and the boot has to be opened. Why carry bombs only in these two places remains a mystery. Cordoning off areas has come to mean stretching a flimsy nylon rope between two light poles, behind which media personnel and self-styled do-gooders wait to crash through at the first sign of some 'development'.

The local administration may have many parking laws but turns a blind eye to all infractions, which means that the commandos are busy trying to move scooters and cars before they can take any action on terrorists holed up in a building. It's absolute hogwash to snigger at developed nations as being sterile and over organized societies and claim that we are vibrant, thanks to the chaos. A chaotic state, it must be recognized, is far more vulnerable to sporadic attacks.

If we are serious about tackling terrorism, then it's not just the strength of the law but our ability to respond to terror which will define success or failure. At the moment with our complete lack of organization and the huge number of soft targets, we are unlikely to shed the dubious status of the most terrorized nation in the world any time soon.

The political economy of terrorism

Terrorism is the premeditated use, or threat to use, of violence by individuals or subnational groups in order to obtain a political or social objective through the intimidation of a large audience beyond that of the immediate victims. Two essential ingredients characterize any modern definition of terrorism: the presence or threat of violence and a political / social motive. Without violence or its threat, terrorists cannot make a political decision maker respond to their demands.

Terrorists broaden their audience beyond their immediate victims by making their actions appear to be random, so that everyone feels anxiety. In contrast to a drive-by shooting on a city street, terrorist acts are not random but well–planned and often well executed attacks where the terrorists account for risks and associated costs as well as possible gains. In addition to violence and a political motive, a minimalist definition hinges on three additional factors: the victim, the perpetrator, and the audience. Of these three, the most controversial is the identity of the victim. Why do terrorists seek such a wide audience? Terrorists want to circumvent the normal political channels / procedures and create political change through threats and violence. Terrorist tactics are more effective in liberal democracies.

Praveen Swami in *Hindu* dt. 17th, Jan. 2009 writes about Lashkar-e-Taiba network in India

Last month, the Jamaat-ud-Dawa's weekly newspaper *Ghazwa* hailed the Mumbai massacre as "an historic victory for the Muslim warriors, who have avenged the atrocities committed by India against its Muslim minority." For weeks now, the world has been seeking to compel Pakistan to dismantle the terror factories which produced those 'warriors.' So far, these efforts have had little success: only a few of the camps run by the Jamaat-ud-Dawa's armed wing, the Lashkar-e-Taiba, have been dismantled; few of its leaders have been arrested. But the most pressing threat to India comes from Lashkar operatives who will not have to cross the oceans or scale the mountains across the Line of Control. Key leaders of Indian Mujahideen — the terrorist network responsible for a string of urban bombings since 2005 — escaped a nationwide police hunt which led to the arrest of over 80 of its operatives in six states. If the Indian Mujahideen is indeed planning further strikes, two men are most likely central to its plans: Riyaz Bhatkal, who organised the quasi-industrial production of the ready-to-assemble ammonium nitrate based 'U'-shaped bombs used in its bombing campaign, and the man tasked by the Lashkar's central commanders to link these units together, Mumbai-based SIMI operative Abdul Subhan Usman Qureshi. Bhatkal, the son of the owner of a leather tanning factory in Mumbai's Kurla area was part of the circle of student Islamists who joined the Students Islamic Movement of India around 1998. Like others in SIMI, Bhatkal believed that the problems confronting India's Muslim were the consequence of secular modernity and that the answer lay in fighting to create an Islamic state. Along with his elder brother Iqbal Bhatkal, a qualified cleric who also practised Unani medicine, Bhatkal became a key figure at SIMI's Mumbai office. SIMI old-timers recall that Bhatkal brothers attended SIMI's last public gathering — a 2001 rally held at Mumbai's Bandra Reclamation ground. Its zeitgeist was incendiary. Osama bin Laden was described as a "true mujahid [Islamic warrior]." Indian Muslims were exhorted to "trample the infidels." Soon after, SIMI was proscribed and the Mumbai Police began knocking on the Bhatkal family's door. Tiring of confrontation with the law, the Bhatkal brothers left for Mangalore. Incensed by the 2003 pogrom in Gujarat, though, Riyaz Bhatkal travelled to Pakistan to train with the Lashkar. Pakistan-based mafioso Amir Raza Khan, who began financing jihadist groups after his brother was killed by the Gujarat Police in 2001, is believed to have paid for the journey, and arranged for the fake travel documents that allowed Bhatkal to transit through Dubai. Back in Mangalore, Bhatkal began to recruit the men who would later form the bomb-manufacture cell of the Indian Mujahideen, mostly small businessmen, like arrested suspects Ahmad Baba Abu Bakr, Ali Mohammad Ahmad, Javed Mohammad Ali and Syed Mohammad Naushad. Iqbal Bhatkal drew other circles of recruits, operating through clerical networks. Mansoor Asghar Peerbhoy, the software engineer who helped design, produce and e-mail several Indian Mujahideen manifestos — and is now expected to testify against his one-time associates—was among them. Kerala's Abdul Sattar, a Kannur resident also known by the alias Sainuddhin, and his long-standing associate Tadiyantavide Nasir, also formed a key part of the circle of south Indian jihadists recruited by the Bhatkal brothers. Both men had cut their political teeth in street battles between followers of the Kerala politician Abdul Nasser Madani — who was recently acquitted of charges of having financed the 1998 serial bombings in Coimbatore by the Islamist terror group al-Umma and Rashtriya Swayamsevak Sangh activists. Sattar, for example, is alleged to have fabricated the pipe-bombs used in a series of 1993 attacks. Later, the men were alleged to have participated in a plot to assassinate former Kerala chief minister EK Nayanar. Sattar and Nasir, the police claim, supplied much of the ammonium nitrate used in the bombs built by Bhatkal in Gujarat. Evidence also exists that the Kerala jihad leaders had sent upwards 40 men for military training at Lashkar camps in Pakistan. In October, four Kerala men training with the Lashkar in the mountains above the north Kashmir town of Kupwara were shot dead by the Jammu and Kashmir Police. One of the four, Abdul Raheem, was Sattar's son-in-law. He had earlier been charged with participating in the 2005 torching of a bus to protest Tamil Nadu's decision to oppose Madani's efforts to secure bail. In the north, similar jihadist modules were forming. In late 2001, Azamgarh resident Mohammad Sadiq Sheikh left for Pakistan. Sheikh, an ideological Islamist linked to SIMI in Uttar Pradesh, had succeeded in making contact with the Lashkar through his brother-in-law, Mujahid Salim — the son of Hyderabad-based Islamist cleric Maulana Abdul Aleem Islahi, who founded the Jamiat-ul-Sheikh Maududi, named after the founder of the Jamaat-e-Islami. Like Bhatkal, Sheikh's travel to Pakistan was arranged through Khan's criminal network. Sheikh, after his return, recruited several figures alleged to have played a key role in the Indian Mujahideen bombings. Indian Mujahideen commander Atif Amin, who was killed in a September shootout with the Delhi Police in Jamia Nagar, is thought to have been trained in Pakistan, as did Mumbai-based Arif Badr Sheikh. So, too, did Shahnawaz Khan, a Lucknow-based Unani doctor whose brother, Mohammad Saif, was arrested during the Jamia Nagar raid. Mumbai's Qureshi, investigators believe, had the critical task of helping these complex, local cells of jihadists knit together into a single unity. His task was complex: in the Ahmedabad attacks, for example, Qureshi mated Bhatkal's bomb-making assets with a group of SIMI operatives raised by computer graphics designer Qayamuddin Kapadia, who in turn provided safe houses and logistical support for Atif Amin's assault team. Like Bhatkal, Qureshi was the son of working class parents who had migrated to Mumbai, in this case from Uttar Pradesh. Like, Bhatkal, he too received technical education. He obtained a diploma in industrial electronics in 1995, and went on to work at several private information technology firms in Mumbai. It is unclear just when Qureshi encountered SIMI, but he was present at the organisation's 1999 convention, a time when he was working on setting up Wipro project to set up an intranet at Bharat Petrochemicals. His links with SIMI deepened over the coming years. In March 2001, Qureshi quit his job at the computer firm Datamatics, recording in a letter of resgination that he had "decided to devote one complete year to pursue religious and spiritual matters." Qureshi is thought to have been trained in Pakistan. Like Bhatkal, he travelled with assistance from Khan's mafia network. From 2005, the Indian jihadists who got trained with the Lashkar initiated a new phase in the Pakistan-based terror group's long-running war against India. Asad Yazdani, a resident of Hyderabad's Toli Chowki area who was among Maulana Nasir's first recruits, carried out a series of strikes starting with the assassination of Gujarat Home Minister Haren Pandya. More often than not, these early operations, like the June, 2005 bombing of the Shramjeevi Express and the March, 2006, attack on the Sankat Mochan temple in Varanasi, relied on cross-border logistical assistance from the Lashkar or Harkat-ul Jihad-e-Islami. In time, their operations became increasingly independent and lethal. Some Mumbai police investigators believe that unidentified Pakistanis who helped execute the July 2006 attacks on the city's suburban train system were not Pakistani at all — but, rather, Amin and other members of the Azamgarh cell. It is certainly possible. Rahil Ahmad Sheikh, a top Indian jihadist who played a key role in sending several men linked with the train bombings to camps in Pakistan – and was sighted at the Lashkar's headquarters in Lahore last year — knew both Bhatkal and Qureshi from their days in SIMI's Mumbai office. In the wake of the Mumbai bombings, the Lashkar came under intense pressure from Pakistan President Pervez Musharraf regime to scale back offensive operations against, India, Lakhvi and other Lashkar commanders, prodded Qureshi, Bhatkal and Sheikh to set up a self-sustaining network in India. On the eve of attacking three court complex buildings in Uttar Pradesh in November, 2007, the three men finally gave their network a name. "Remember my friends," Jamaat-ud-Dawa chief Hafiz Mohammad Saeed had said in a February 5, 2007 speech, delivered not long after the discussions that led to the formation of the Indian Mujahideen "that the jihad has been ordained by Allah". "It is not an order of a general," he continued, "that can be started one day and stopped the other day. Our jihad in Kashmir will end when all the Hindus will be destroyed in India." Saeed's threats may be psychotic, but he has demonstrated they are made in earnest, and delivered on reason enough for India to pay close attention.

TERRORISM IN KASHMIR

Former Governor of J&K and an eminent administrator Shri Jagmohan has written about the menace of terrorism in Jammu

& Kashmir. He states that even in the mid-sixties of the last century, strands of contemporary terrorism were visible in Kashmir. During the five years, from January 1965 to January 1971, no less than 80 underground cells and espionage rings, including Al Fatah, Al Baro and Al Kashmir, were in the Valley. In this period huge arms and ammunition were seized by the police. The subversive activities continued in the Kashmir Valley, even after the Indo-Pak War of 1965 and the Tashkent Declaration of 1966.

Al Fatah

The period (1965-71) was dominated by Al Fatah, which derived its name from an Arab guerilla organisation committed to the liberation of Palestine. It alludes to a Quranic verse which implies "assistance from God and imminent success". Its main organiser was Gulam Rasool Jehangir. In course of time, he secured support of some young men whom he was able to motivate with a great deal of success. The main objective of Al Fatah was to indulge in espionage, bomb explosions, and other acts of subversion. Its strategy included destruction of holy places, such as 'Maqdoom Saheb Ki Ziarat', so as to arouse communal passion. Its top leaders were guided, trained and motivated by officers of Pakistan Intelligence. Following a terrorism-related case near Hazratbal, the investigators detected the hand of Al Fatah and arrested its main leaders. The investigators also found that a large quantity of arms had been kept by Saleem Jehangir at Charar-e-Sharief. It was also discovered that there was a diabolical plan of kidnapping and assassinating VIPs, including Chief Minister and Ministers, who were considered to be easy targets during the elections of 1971.

Till the beginning of the second half of the last century, Kashmir's Islamic ethos were shaped by the liberal order of Sufis and Rishis. Unfortunately, this liberal order was gradually undermined, first by the selfish politics and then by the forces let loose by Jama'at-e-Islami and other fundamentalist organisations. They never hesitated to use Islam if found it expedient to do so.

Who declared in the true style of a religious leader that it would be sin to offer funeral prayers, namaz-e-janaza for Muslims who were members.

Jama'at-e-Islami

The Jama'at-e-Islami' of Jammu and Kashmir is a separate and independent body. But it is on the same wavelength as of the Jama'at-e-Islami of Pakistan. It denounces what it calls 'Indian colonialism' and 'Brahminical imperialism'. It advocates establishment of Nizam-e-Mustafa in accordance with Maudoodi's ideas and wants Kashmiri society to be re-fashioned in accordance with the principles and ideas of the 'Shariat'.

Jama'at-e-Islami was founded in India in 1938 by Sayyid Abul Aala Maudoodi. He developed the concept of Nizam-e-Mustafa, that is, the system which had been enunciated by Prophet Mohammad. He wanted total supremacy to be given to the Quran and 'Sunna'. He held that political sovereignty vested in God; that the ruler, who could rule only on behalf of God, should be the most virtuous Muslim and the Ummah (Muslim community) must elect only such a person as the ruler. He denounced nationalism and pinned his faith in the supranational character of Islam. He said: "Muslim nationalism is as contradictory a term as a chaste prostitute". He wanted to mould the entire social, moral, political and economic system of the world in accordance with the tenets of Islam.

Because of the Jama'at-e-Islami's operation at social, educational and cultural levels in Jammu and Kashmir and growing number of its workers, it had always more strength beneath the surface than above it. Its electoral performances of the past are no indication of its real hold on the mindscape of the Muslims. Moreover, in the 1977 and 1983 elections, the National Conference, by its very communal, parochial and pro-Pak stance, virtually displaced the appeal of the Jama'at-e-Islami. It did exactly what the Jama'at-e-Islami was intending to do. The youth organisations, which later on aligned with Jama'at-e-Islami, were, in essence, no different from the youth organisations which aligned with the political party.

All this led to creation of an environment which was favourable for the growth of subversive and terrorism-oriented activities. From August 15, 1983 onwards, a series of bombs explosions occurred in the Valley. In connection with one such explosion, four suspects Iqbal Qureshi, Altaf Qureshi, Altaf Mahajan and Majad Lala, were picked up by the police, Iqbal Qureshi was the brother of Hashmi Qureshi who had hijacked an Indian Airlines Fokker Friendship plane in 1971.

On October 13, 1983, highly deplorable acts of subversion were witnessed during the one-day international cricket match between India and the West Indies. The moment the aforesaid approach ceased and old permissive attitudes returned in mid-1989. On July 13 1989, Tikka Lal Taploo, an advocate and vice-president of BJP, was shot dead near his house. Judge N.K. Ganjoo, who had sentenced Magbool Butt was killed on Novermber 4, 1989, in broad daylight at busy Hari Singh Street. Pran Nath Butt, a noted journalist was done to death on December 29, 1989. The murder of these three prominent leaders of the Kashmiri Pandit community was in line with the terrorists policy of killing one and frightening one thousand. The objective was to secure the exodus of the Pandits from the Valley. No one was arrested and tried for these crimes. The state virtually did not exist. Terrorism reappeared. Inexcusably, no action was taken even when prominent leaders of Pandit community were killed. Release of Dr. Rubaiya Sayeed daughter of then Union Home Minister, who was earlier kidnapped was obtained by surrendering to the demand of the militants.

Effect of Afghanistan war

The war in Afghanistan (1979-89) had made the ISI one of the most dangerous and powerful intelligence organisations in the world. The United States had placed in its hand huge resources, Besides vast sums of money, it got a massive stock of sophisticated weapons and communication equipment. All these resources were given to the ISI to train and motivate Afghan Mujahideens to wage a furious and fanatical war against the troops of "Godless Soviet Union". But the ISI, clever and crafty as it has always been, sliced off a good part of the finances and equipment. According to a report of the US Congress, as much as 60 per cent of equipment was, directly or indirectly, kept by the ISI for its own purposes. The ISI was also strengthened by way of the experience it got in waging *a* subversive war in neighbouring countries. A large number of Mujahideens, from countries like Egypt, Algeria, Tunisia and Saudi Arabia, too, come in its fold. *The Times* had rightly noted: "The Afghan war left behind a virtual band of Islamic mercenaries, highly motivated, militarily hardened and ready to take action almost anywhere in the cause of Islam". All this wherewithal - finances, equipment, experience and motivation and trained manpower - enabled the ISI to spin an extensive network of subversion and terrorism in Kashmir. According to a document titled, *The New Islamist International,* prepared in January 1994 by the Task Force of the US House of Representatives: The mere size of Pakistani training programme is telling. In 'Azad Kashmir' alone, there are 13 permanent, 18 temporary and 8 joint training camps. Islamist indoctrination is provided by Jama'at-e-Islami of Pakistan... Highly trained terrorists of the Jamiat-e-Tulba, were sent in to establish a country-wide support system. They developed a professional infiltration and exfiltration route for their operatives via Nepal and used that country as a site for their meetings and consultations with Pakistani and Arab terrorism and subversion experts. While in India, the terrorists relied on support from members of such organisations as the Indian Student Islamic Movement.

CONCLUSION

Men and women of courage fascinates us. Stories of people who took brave decisions in the service of great causes entrance us, especially when more comfortable and far less dangerous alternatives were open to them. But what separates these people of courage from the rest of us and makes their lives and achievements so remarkable is that they were prepared to endure great sacrifices and persists, some of them for many years, against the odds and in the face of the great adversity. They are for us examples and icon, at once daunting and cherished. Their stories live on and inspire us.

Brave and courageous man remains a hero without a grave. But as long as humanity remembers those days his name will live as a symbol of courage in the face of seemingly invincible evil. He stands firm, he refuses to be intimidated, he resists, knowing that in dark times what we do makes a difference. The good we do lives after us and it's the greatest thing that does. Years ago the sages said a single human life is like a universe. Save a life and you save a world. Change a life and you begin to change the world.

Sir Winston Churchil has said. "Courage is the first of human qualities because it is the quality which guarantees all others".

Courage is not absence of fear but the mastery of it.

What is it that makes some men and women take difficult decisions and do the right thing against the odds when easier and far less dangerous alternatives are open to them? Why is it that some people, like the under-cover military heroes working for SOE in occupied France or the passengers of the United 93 flight on 9/11, have the courage to dare?

The problem with hatred and violence is that they intensify the fears of the oppressors and leave them less ashamed of their prejudices towards oppressed. In the guilt and confusion confronting our society, violence only adds to the chaos. It deepens the brutality and increases the bitterness. Violence is the antithesis of creativity and wholeness. It destroys community and makes brotherhood impossible.

There is an urgent need to go against the prevailing intellectual consensus, largely derived from the Western tradition, that the only way to turn around public utilities which are not performing up to the expected level is through corporatisation, privatization, retrenchment, hike in user fees etc. The first lesson to absorb is the domestic political context and then things would fall in place. The model of inclusive reform based on full recovery of costs through user fees may be applied to turn around sectors like power, water supply, irrigation and urban transport. However there is no single bullet of reforms that will work in all these sectors. Each has its own specific political and social context so one cannot take a template approach to reforming these sectors.

The bureaucracy must respect the political mandate to begin with. Mutual contempt or skepticism must be replaced by mutual trust between politician and the bureaucrat. What we need today is a cadre of thinkers and managers who look at the pressing politico-economic problems of the day from an Indian specific prism. This is the time to evolve our own thinking process that is rooted in our own cultural context. As the western world goes deeper into a recession and grapples with its own long held belief systems, India is required to think hard and evolve its domestic strategies to keep the GDP growth rate constant at 7-8 per cent.

We should not think about delivering a fiscal stimulus package. We need to think a thousand small ideas in other sectors such as power, water, public transport, irrigation etc., which will aggregate to become one big idea. It may just be easier to create a consensus among the people, politicians and bureaucrats to deliver a thousand small ideas to accelerate growth in the economy.

Combating Terrorism

Priority should be given by the Government to control terrorism, which is spreading its tentacles alaround. It is good that LTTE in Sri Lanka has been demolished by killing its leader Prabhakaran and his son by the Sri Lankan Army fully equipped with latest Chinese weapons.

Every constitutional order provides for modifications in law to enable the state to face challenges to its unity and integrity and the security of its citizens. In fact, the entire criminal justice system which gives the state the power to use force against its own citizens, going even to the extent of resorting to killings, is designed for this purpose. In case of emergency, situations such as an internal rebellion or external aggression, the state's power to use force is further enhanced, but with suitable checks to prevent abuse or denial of the due process of law. In the process, what happens is a fresh balancing of the interests of liberty and security — both of which are the foundations of the rule of law in a constitutional system. Without security there is no liberty or freedom; and without liberty and freedom, security is not worth preserving for democratic societies. The challenge, therefore, is to find an acceptable balance between the two and to ensure that the government keeps within the limits set by law in the exercise of its authority.

The Indian Constitution, born in difficult times after Partition, does provide for a legal regime which can accommodate reasonable restrictions on liberty, the standards of which can vary depending on the gravity of the challenge and the risks involved for basic rights and constitutional values. We have an independent judiciary to test the constitutionality of the standards set by the laws and to ensure the accountability of those who exercise public authority under those laws.

It is only in this framework that one can appreciate the recent enactments on terrorism and seek to understand the fresh balancing between liberty and security that is attempted through them. Of course, opinions may differ as they always do in a democratic set-up. But partisan considerations should not be allowed to cloud judgment.

Though laws, no matter how harsh they are, cannot by themselves prevent terrorist attacks, they can help in the successful investigation and prosecution of cases against terrorists and those who aid and abet terrorist acts. Therefore the need for special laws to combat terrorism cannot be under estimated. However, equally important are institutions set up to implement terrorism-related laws, and the level of motivation and competence of persons appointed to run those institutions. The problem lies with the implementation of laws and abuse of powers conferred on the authorities under the special laws.

The record in this regard has been far from satisfactory, to say the least. Popular criticism against these laws has been based more on the manner in which they are implemented than on any modifications in the laws and procedures. Had the regular criminal justice system performed its task with reasonable results, there would have been no need for special laws or institutions to deal with terrorist acts. In the long run, only good governance can control terrorism. Meanwhile, as a temporary measure, the country needs special laws that empower the government to combat terrorism. Hard crimes and soft justice cannot co-exist for long if security is desired.

The fight against "terror" is larger and more complex than the challenge of dealing with terrorists. The former requires more statesmanship and good governance. The latter demands legislative and administrative reforms to plug loopholes in criminal law and the criminal justice administration. In this regard, the reform of the police and the prosecution machinery has been identified as an essential step. Reforms are to achieve professionalisation and capacity building. Specific recommendations in this regard are already on the table and the Supreme Court had given direction to implement certain minimum measures. The lack of political will, the fear of the unknown, and manipulation by vested interests in the administration are reportedly holding up the changes in the statutes.

Three distinct functions are involved in combating terrorism. They relate to preempting and preventing, containing and managing, and investigating and prosecuting. There may be a need for a convergence of these three functions at operational levels. The challenge before the government is managing the three-fold counter-terrorism mechanism for optimum results. A management plan and a management team are to be put in place with adequate powers and resources as some of the developed countries have done. The Constitution will not come in the way of mounting such an effort with appropriate legislative support.

The most important change brought about recently is in respect of streamlining the investigation and prosecution of terrorist offences at the Central level. The establishment of the National Investigation Agency under the NIA Act of 2008 is the first step towards effective handling of terrorism related offences. Parliament passed the law with near unanimity, which indicates the willingness of different political parties ruling the States to enable the Centre to act on the issue. Combating terrorism is a joint responsibility of Central, State and local governments. Timely accurate intelligence and up-to-date information regarding terrorist elements are essential to evolve strategies to counter terrorist activity. This requires multi-agency coordination and time-bound action which only an empowered central body having regional and local field offices with instant connectivity can accomplish.

Similarly, a dedicated team of highly motivated, well trained and fully professionalised officers supported by adequate resources, equipment and authority alone can take timely action to combat terror.

In the last two decades, the scale of insurgencies, separatist movements, etc., have assumed a completely new dimension. The meaning of governance here is very different from the normal, where personnel and their families are under threat to life. The psychological, physical and material requirements of dealing with these situations are unusual. The picture is complicated by 'political' angles and human rights questions. Enough thought had not been given to understanding the ramifications of these challenges to the rule of law and to national integrity, and to evolving institutions and processes for effective governance in such situations. What is needed is an overseeing body, which did not change with every political swing. There is lack of will and support for hard steps from the highest levels: The police should have full authority, and as recommended by the National Police Commission, state security commissions, with representatives from different walks of life, could be constituted as watchdogs to oversee its actions.

There is need for seriousness of the present loss of faith in the integrity, impartiality and efficiency of the All India Services. No doubt that the IAS, the IPS and other Group-A officers are performing highly significant, continuing national-scale duties but it is necessary to find out what has gone wrong and why. There are three stages in the decline of these services—commitment to a party during the 1970s (including the Emergency), politicisation and hobnobbing with politicians during the 1980s, and becoming part of the criminal-politician nexus in the 1990s (as stressed in the Vohra Committee Report, leading to a sort of parallel government). The external factor of galloping population, which was not being tackled effectively, has not only led to pressures and shortages, but also contributed to the falling standards of service, and expansion of government size. The officers could be blamed for their own declining standards of conduct as professionals for many undesirable developments. A few ambitious officers, flouting formal lines of command and communication, have gained extraordinary access to politicians, and acting as an extra-constitutional authority. They are actively advising against state interests and aggravating the caste divide. Many officers, without being under any compulsion to do so, have developed a servile manner and style. There should be focus on three specific subjects namely, (i) reform from within; (ii) provide external stimuli for reform; and (iii) reform IAS-IPS relations. Service Associations, should rise above ad hoc, sectarian, and social roles and delve into these subjects of state and public interest issues; where required, the IAS and IPS should develop joint assessments also.

Obstacles in reforms

Of all the components of civil services, the police of late has grown most in importance. Whereas, after the ascendancy of forces of globalisation, marketisation and deregulations, other civil services have seen reduction in their functions, the police has added immensely to its role and responsibilities. With substantial withdrawal of the state from industries, trade and other areas of the economy, increasing trends towards privatisation and even disinvestment of existing public enterprises, the administrative and economic services have been losing direct control over public affairs. On the other hand, consequent to the need for enforcing new laws and regulations to deal with those who are out to misuse the new opportunities provided by new technologies and new environment of liberalisation, the police has added many more activities to its sphere.

The mounting waves of terrorism, subversion, Maoism-Naxalism and communal and castes animosities have created another set of complex problems for the police to deal with. The tension and conflict-ridden society in India today and the growing intrusion of criminal elements in her political power-structure are throwing up challenges which are of its own kind. All in all, the Indian police is in a turbulent sea of trouble and is being buffeted from all sides, finding it extremely difficult to remain afloat. Coming to the fast changing crime-scenario all over the world, powerful international criminal groups now work outside national or international law. They include traffickers in drugs, money-laundering, illegal trade in arms, including trade in nuclear materials and the smuggling of precious metals and other commodities. These criminal elements exploit both the new liberal international economic order and the different approaches and practices of States. They command vast sums of money, which they use to suborn State officials. Millions of dollars could be sent in a short time from one country to another electronically, making it difficult to detect the links in the long chain of devious transaction. A number of new avenues of generating illegal income have also opened up and facilitated the emergence of sophisticated networks of crime. According to the World Watch Report on Global Security (2005): Transnational crime syndicates distribute harmful materials, weapons, and drugs, they exploit local community and disrupt fragile eco-systems, and they control significant economic resources. In 2003, transnational crime syndicates may have grossed up to $2 trillion — more than all national economies except the United States, Japan and Germany. The bulk of crime syndicates' revenue comes from drug trafficking. Sales of illegal drugs annually ranged anywhere from $300 billion to $500 billion. Perhaps one of the most tragic business that transnational criminal organisations are involved in is the trafficking of humans. While the number is difficult to know for sure, the US State Department estimates that at least 600,000 - 800,000 people are sold internationally each year — exploited for labour, sexual services, or even the removal of their kidneys or other organs for transplant purposes.

The small arms, too, have proliferated. It has been estimated by the United Nations that the arsenal of these arms in the world today exceeds 640 million, out of which about 226 million are with the armed forces and law-enforcing agencies. The remaining 414 million are in the hands of private individuals, licensed or unlicensed. There has been a virtual flood of small, light and easily portable weapons of destruction which makes even the most well-administered state vulnerable to frequent disruption and disorder. The growing violence of the times has been made possible by what Eric Hobshawn has described as "the extraordinary explosion in the global supply and availability to private persons and groups of sufficiently cheap, powerfully destructive armaments capable of being handled by anybody." And this he has attributed to the propensity of the present day businessmen to make quick money. "Every decade since 1960 has seen the number of firms producing them rise. In 1994 there were three hundred companies in fifty-two countries in the small arms business, 25 percent more than in the mid-1980s; in 2001 the number was estimated at five hundred. Kalashnikovs are a most formidable form of small arms; anything up to 125 million of them are circulating in the world today. As for handguns and knives, who can count them?" Hobshawn goes on to opine: "War in the twenty-first century is not likely to be as murderous as it was in the twentieth. But armed violence, creating disproportionate suffering and loss, will remain omnipresent and endemic - occasionally epidemic - in a large part of the world. The prospect of a century of peace is remote." Cyber crime, including use of computer viruses to destroy data and cause breakdown of communication systems, is proving to be another menace. The nation's power plants, fuel supplies, space satellites and factories could be easily brought to a halt. The Internet weapon could be as deadly as other weapons of mass destruction. At the end of 2001, there were 71,000 computer viruses identified as in the wild. The hate-sites are also being put up on the net to arouse mass frenzy against the perceived adversary. Clearly, the Indian police today has so many fronts to keep vigil upon, so many hitherto uncharted courses to traverse and so many inner layers of white collar-crimes to peep into that nothing less than a total transformation of its organisational structure and technological wherewithal would do. In its working, a very high degree of professional competence would have to be injected.

Unfortunately, while the need is for a radical improvement in various spheres of police administration, the conditions with regard to most of them are taking a turn for the worse. The social milieu remains as unfavourable as before. The political environment is having a negative impact. And growing culture of amassing maximum money in the minimum time is causing a cynical disregard for values of justice, truth and rectitude. The police, we tend to forget, is a part of the social milieu; it does not function in a vacuum. We seldom look into our disposition and shirk our responsibilities as a citizen. We show marked unwillingness to tender evidence in a court of law even when we are an eye witness to a crime. Quite a few of us show little compunction of conscience by turning hostile for a consideration or out of fear of the accused. Moreover, we as a society, excel in practising double standards. "Janus-like", to use the expression of Ben Whitaker, "..we have always turned two faces towards a policeman. We resent him when he enforces law in our case, yet demand his dismissal when he does not enforce it elsewhere. We offer him bribes, yet denounce his corruption".

Whereas the social environment continues to be uncongenial, the style of our politics has contributed another set of negativities. "The professional autonomy of the police force in India", bemoaned late N.A. Palkhiwala, "has been completely destroyed by political directives and political influences." As early as 1959, the Kerala Police Reorganisation Committee had observed: "The result of partisan interference is often reflected in lawless enforcement of laws, inferior service and in general decline of police prestige." The comments of the National Police Commission (1977-80) in this respect are equally pertinent: "What started as a normal interaction between the politician and services with the avowed objective of better awareness of public expectations, soon degenerated into different forms of intercession, intervention and interference with malafide objectives, unconnected with public interest."

The cultural values, too, are getting further debased on account of increasing weakness for wealth. Excessive materialism is destroying what little values of fairness and honest work remain in the people. The means do not count; the end of gaining power and pelf is all that matters.

It is the unhealthy social, political and cultural ethos of the nation, and not merely the internal inadequacies of the police set up that are responsible for the numerous maladies from which it suffers. Neither has the national leadership nor our civil society shown clear understanding of this phenomenon. It is, in fact, a measure of the superficialities with which India has lived through the last sixty years that she does not even consider why the reports submitted by various high level and earnest Reforms Commissions and Committees, and the observations and recommendations made therein, have remained unattended, and why, instead of generating the requisite implementational will, the only measure that is thought of to meet worsening conditions is to appoint yet another Commission or Committee.

In the meanwhile, the maladies continue to make deeper inroads into the system. It should, therefore, not cause surprise to anyone to note that, with the passage of time, the disposition to misuse political authority and make the police bend the law in favour of the ruling clique has become more pronounced. And so has the willingness of a large number of police personnel to ingratiate themselves with their political master by resorting to irregularities and illegalities.

While the increased misuse of the police for personal and political purposes has shattered whatever image of impartiality it had been left with, its general performance with regard to maintenance of law and order and as an agency for investigating and prosecuting cases has suffered a further decline. Notwithstanding the fact that a large number of cases are not reported to the police, or not registered by it, 3 IPC crimes and 6 special and local laws crimes are, on an average, committed every minute in the country, as per records of the Home Ministry's journal, *Crime in India*. Only 30 percent of the cases registered are sent for trial. Even they remain pending for years.

In the words of Justice Y.K. Sabharwal, former Chief Justice of India, "the criminal justice delivery system appears to be on the verge of collapse". Earlier, in 2003, the Committee on Reforms of Criminal justice system, had observed: "Violent and organised crimes have become the order of the day. As chances of conviction are remote, crime has become a profitable business. Life has become unsafe and people live in constant fear. Law and order situation has deteriorated and the citizens have lost confidence in the criminal justice system." Similar views were expressed by the National Commission to review the working of the Constitution, which submitted its report to the government in 2002: "The greatest asset of the police in investigation of crimes and maintenance of law and order is the confidence of the people. Today, such public confidence is at the lowest level."

REQUIREMENT OF STRICT RULE

India is also a peculiar case of a soft and permissive state with stern and stringent laws. It combines the disadvantages of both. While, on the one hand, it suffers from the fallouts of softness and permissiveness, on the other, it is subjected to severe criticism for having draconian laws. Neither are the objectives of strong laws attained nor the country's image effectively protected from the onslaught of India-baiters and human rights bodies.

Take, for example, the case of Kashmir. After it was badly hit by Pakistan-sponsored terrorism in mid-1989, stringent laws like the Terrorist and Disruptive Activities (Prevention) Act, 1987 (TADA), were enacted. But the manner in which these laws were enforced showed how weak was the resolve of the rulers of the country to combat terrorism, how poor was their capacity for implementation and how selfishly disposed were they to sacrifice national interests for short-term political gains.

During the six years' period (1990-96), despite hundreds of heinous crimes, not a single dangerous terrorist was convicted under the TADA—not even the self-confessed killers of the four officers of the Indian Air Force, the murderers of the Kashmir University Vice Chancellor Mushir-ul-Haq, the Doordarshan Station Director Lasa Kaul and Awami Action Committee leader Mirwaiz Maulvi Farooq. The extent of the softness of the Indian state can also be seen from the 2006 report of the US State Department. It says "During 1988 to 2002, there have been 13 convictions of terrorists, though thousands have become victims of their crime."

But as briefly indicated above, the factor that is damaging most the standing and image of the police is the increasing tendency of its political masters to misuse their powers to serve their partisan ends. More often than not, it is their orders, mostly oral, and not the provisions of law, that determine the course of investigation or prosecution. When they or their supporters are involved in criminal cases, they ensure that these cases are scuttled at some stage or the other. On the other hand, they go out of the way to harass their political opponents, sometimes going to the extent of instituting false cases.

To minimize misuse of power by political authorities with regard to functioning of the police and to prevent arbitrary transfers and suspensions, the Supreme Court, in its judgment, delivered on September 22, 2006, on a Public Interest Litigation, WP 310/1996, issued the following main directions to the Central and State governments:

(i) A State Security Commission should be set up in every state to ensure that "the State Government does not exercise unwarranted influence or pressure on the State police and for laying guidelines so that the State police always acts according to the laws of the land and the Constitution of the country."

(ii) The above Watchdog Commission shall comprise Chief Minister or Home Minister as its head, Director-General Police as its secretary and other members who shall be chosen on any of the models recommended by the National Human Rights Commission, the Ribeiro Committee and Sorabji Committee.

(iii) The Director-General of Police shall be selected by the State government from amongst the three senior most officers who have been empanelled for promotion to that rank by the Union Public Service Commission; once selected, he should have a minimum tenure of two years.

(iv) All other police officers on operational duties in the field shall also have a minimum tenure of two years.

(v) There shall be a Police Establishment Board headed by the Director-General of Police, in each state "which shall decide" all transfers, postings, promotions and other service related matters of officers of and below the rank of Deputy Superintendent of Police".

(vi) The said Police Establishment Board shall also be concerned to make appropriate recommendations regarding the posting and transfer of officers of and above the rank of Superintendent of Police.

While issuing the above directions, the Supreme Court had taken into consideration the recommendations made by various high level Commissions and Committees appointed from time to time. The Court noted that these recommendations "have remained only on paper without any action" and observed:

"Having regard to (i) the gravity of the problem; (ii) the urgent need for preservation and strengthening of rule of law; (iii) pendency of even this petition for the last 10 years; (iv) the fact that various commissions and committees have made recommendations on similar lines for introducing reforms in the police set-up in the country; and (v) total uncertainty as to when the police reforms would be introduced, we think that there cannot be any further wait."

Nevertheless, the real issue remains: Would the directions of the Supreme Court have any impact in practice, and would it ever be possible to ensure that the police acts only in accordance with the laws and Constitution and that the political executive is not able, under the cover of democratic control and supervision, to make the police a pawn in its power-game — a game which is now being played with increasing ruthlessness?

Reform measures

The corruption in police is of different type than other departments. Here lower officers directly dealing with public take the bribe and pass on to their higher officers. Whereas in other departments sometimes higher officer takes bribe directly.

There should be one point entry for recruitment in police instead of class-I, class-II and class-III. Anyone desiring to enter police should enter at one point and gain experience of basic works and by dint of his qualification and ability should get promotion to higher rank at periodical time.

The colonial system as prevalent prior to independence is being still followed in police that is "to work to please the master".

First, keeping in view the growing complexity and variety of crimes which require, apart from high professional and technical skills, mental and intellectual calibre of very high order, the police cadres for various levels of officers and ranks should be substantially upgraded and made more attractive in terms of emoluments and career prospects. Highly trained and specialised sub-cadres, within the overall cadre, should also be developed to handle the technical equipment and deal with the subversive elements whose activities are increasing both within and outside the country and whose operations are becoming more subtle and technology-oriented.

Secondly, besides setting up the State Security Commissions and the Police Establishment Boards, Government should, on the basis of the recommendations made by various Commissions and Committees, such as the National Police Commission (1977-80), Law Commission's Reports number 152 (1994) and 154 (1996), the J.F. Ribeiro Committee Report (1998), the Padmanabhaiah Committee Report (2000), justice VS. Malimath Committee (2002) and National Commission to Review the Working of the Constitution (2002), evolve anew mechanism to avoid judicial delays to secure substantial reduction in the rate of acquittal and also to impart victim orientation to criminal-justice administration. Institutional arrangements should also be made to insulate 'the police from politics' and to ensure that the policeman acts as an agent and servant "of the law and the law alone". The model Police Bill, recommended by Soli Sorabjee Committee to replace the Police Act of 1861, should also be accepted by the State governments and new laws framed with slight changes that the local conditions may warrant.

Thirdly, the work pertaining to investigation, which "requires patience, skill, long range efforts and expertise of a high order", should be separated from the work of maintaining law and order which calls for "very quick action on the spot, faculty of immediate response, firmness of mind and a decisive approach". After separation, the entire police machinery relating to investigation and prosecution should be placed under a statutory Criminal Justice Commission which would also keep a watch over the state of prisons and the manner in which criminal courts deal with cases, particularly those relating to under-trials which constitute about 65 percent of the total number of prisoners in Indian jails.

Fourthly, certain offences, such as those relating to terrorism, subversion, espionage, money laundering and arms and drug trafficking, should be declared as federal offences and entrusted to an independent federal agency for investigation and prosecution. The superintendence and control over the entire work of Central

Bureau of Investigation should be placed under the Central Vigilance Commission which has now been given statutory status under the Central Vigilance Act, 2003.

Fifthly, the work handled by various intelligence agencies, including those of the armed forces, should be effectively coordinated at the level of the National Security Council. Special attention should be paid to the need for prompt upgradation of technology, so as to keep the intelligence agency always ahead of those elements who are engaged in hatching conspiracies against the nation. By introducing latest techniques of connectivities like WI-Max and WI-F1, the communication system of the police could be put in top gear. Data about hard criminals, including finger-prints and DNA, could be centralised for online transmission to all police stations.

Sixthly, it is time that we ended distrust of the police as an institution. If we expect the Indian police to function as effectively and efficiently as in countries like the U.K., our criminal courts, too, need to develop a more realistic attitude and not insist on perfect proof. In this connection, justice V Krishna Iyer has pertinently observed: "Judicial insistence for perfect proof accounts for police presentation of fool-proof concoction... Why fake up? Because the court asks for manufacture to make truth, look truth. No, we must be realistic. We should also learn to applaud warmly the excellent services which the Indian Police have rendered on quite a few occasions. The Delhi Police, for example, did a remarkable job during the Asian Games, despite heavy odds. Compare its performance with that of the Munich Police during the Olympics of 1972 when 11 Israeli athletes were kidnapped and killed by terrorists. Recently, after a study of the working of 450 police stations in 23 countries, including Belgium, Brazil, Canada, UK and USA, Jaipur's Shipra Path has been rated as the best police station.

Seventhly, the Indian State must shed its soft and permissive attitude. Both the Union and State governments must learn to rise above narrow considerations and take firm steps to nip in the bud all mischief pertaining to law and order, subversion and terrorism.

The criminalization of politics has a direct relation to rapid politicization of the police force. Corrupt police officers help ganglords and anti-social elements, patronized by parties or individuals. Politicians require money and muscle power to win elections. The ganglords supply this in abundant measure, in return for sanction to operate freely. This permission is difficult to obtain if the police chief is a man of integrity, But if he is corrupt or owes favours to politicians, then permission is readily given. The only persons who suffer because of this unholy nexus between the police, politicians and criminals are members of the public, who have to live in an atmosphere of perpetual insecurity because of the reluctance of the politicians and police to control the activities of the anti-socials and criminals.

Gang wars, large-scale smuggling, bootlegging and gambling syndicates all emanate from this nexus. Since the system has evolved to keep politicians concerned in power, there can be no relief for the common man. If another party is elected to form the government, its members very soon get immersed in this system.

White-collar crime is increasing rapidly with the spread of technology and the advent of the consumer society. Government regulations have boosted white-collar crime. Businessmen are constantly finding ways of bribing politicians and bureaucrats to obtain licences for ventures, or they are busy devising means to evade taxes and in the process, engendering a whole new Culture of disrespect for the law. Criminal minds have adopted ingenious methods to get rich quickly. The scams that we read about almost every day in the newspapers are a manifestation of this trend. A hundred times more money is lost in white-collar crime than through crimes of violence. The loss to the economy is immense. Yet, the middle classes do not shun such criminals. They do not hesitate to invite them for public functions. They will not invite bank robbers or petty thieves though they commit offences for survival, and not because they want more wealth than they already have, as do the white-collar criminals.

It is extremely important for the police to project the image of 'a friend of the people'. People means good and law-abiding people. If the policeman is seen as an enemy of the law-breakers, particularly the leaders of organized crime syndicates, it will do his image a world of good. Unfortunately, the public perception is exactly the opposite. The policeman is seen as a friend of antisocial elements who ply him with money and other gifts.

Turning off the tap

The Government may be dithering on a stringent anti-terror law, but it has taken an aggressive stance to turn off the tap on foreign funds that fuel terrorism in India. The Ministry of Home Affairs (MHA), which monitors foreign funds being received by over 32,000 registered non governmental organisations (NGOs), has clamped down on the erring and dubious ones from the bunch.

To begin with, it has quietly started "religion profiling" of the organisations to keep a close watch on their activities. In a bid to not appear anti-minority, the government has directed officials of the Foreigners' Division to segregate all religious organisations—Hindu, Muslim and Christian. The ministry wants to ensure that Rs 7,000 crore that comes into the country officially as charity is not used for anti-national purposes, including terror-funding.

In a swift move that cuts across religious and regional barriers, the Home Ministry has also banned 44 organisations from receiving funds for life. These include several outfits which claimed to be working in the religious and social sectors. Among them: Saraswati Charitable Trust, Delhi; Association Madras Church of Christ, Chennai; Jameah Rashidiyah Trust, Surat; Islamiya College, Kozhikode; Jammu and Kashmir Muslim Conference, Srinagar; and Jamai Atul Falah, Azamgarh.

There are 11 other associations whose accounts have been frozen. "it would not be right to pick out organisations only of a particular religion. Many Islamic organisations have been under the scanner for long due to the apprehension that they may be diverting their funds for spreading terror," a senior home ministry official said. Several Christian organisations, which have been the biggest recipients of foreign funds over the last few years, are also under close watch. Some of the organisations which receive large amounts of foreign funds are the Chennai-based World Vision of India, and Caritas India and Churches Auxiliary for Social Action, both headquartered in Delhi.

Although all recipients are categorised as social, cultural, economic, educational or religious, there are very few who actually list themselves under the religious category. Sources say that in the absence of a streamlined Foreign Contributions (Regulation) Act (FCRA), the ministry had problems in taking action against the doubtful organisations. The FCRA, 1976, has become outdated and needed to be strengthened. More of a national security legislation, the FCRA is weak on issues like tracking the source and utilisation of foreign donations. To replace it with a provision with more teeth, a Foreign Contributions (Regulation) Bill, 2006, was framed but it is still to replace the FCRA. After much delay and going through a Group of Ministers, headed by the home minister, it was introduced in the Rajya Sabha. But instead of being cleared, it was sent to the Parliamentary Standing Committee of the Home Ministry. And that is where it remains. But BJP MP Sushma Swaraj, who heads the committee, told *India Today* once that the panel's deliberations were complete and the report was almost final.

According to former External Affairs Minister Pranab Mukherjee, the Bill was aimed at checking "activities undertaken by unscrupulous elements in the garb of overt welfare schemes and projects". The Government is keen to ensure, he explained, that associations engaged in anti-national and illegal activities are weeded out, and at the same time, genuine NGOs engaged in developmental and welfare work are not harassed. However, with the future of the Bill uncertain, the Foreigners' Division, in the meantime, is trying to do the best it can. "The reported foreign contributions of Rs 7,000 crore are just the tip of the iceberg. An equal amount of money, if not more, could be going unreported since half the organisations have failed to submit their records for scrutiny."

What's worse is that nearly 9,000 NGOs have not submitted their account books for the past three years. All that the ministry can do is put the perennial defaulters on a prior permission list which means that they have to seek its permission every time before accepting a foreign donation. "If they want their names to be off the list, they will have to show all their account books. They will be properly scrutinised and only if they are in perfect order will their names be cleared," the official said. Names of another 24 organisations were added to the long prior permission list. These include Abul Kalam Azad Islamic Awakening Centre of much-in-the-news Jamia Nagar in Delhi. The most stringent action that the ministry could take in the given circumstances was to ban organisations from accepting funds forever, or report some organisations to the CBI for a detailed inquiry. The MHA has reported 17 outfits to the CBI. In its present form, the FCRA does not even have the authority to regulate bank accounts. It is proposed in the new Bill that an institution be allowed to have only one bank account—declared to the Government to receive foreign donations. It could be allowed more accounts only to disburse the amount for various projects. A long haul is just beginning.

Revive the Indian police leadership

More than anything else, the government needs to revive the Indian police leadership, which has over the years declined and in some cases appears to be in a stupor. They have not stood up to politicians and bureaucrats when needed. For that matter, morale of the police force has been dented by political and bureaucratic interference. The government must inquire into this state of affairs and determine for himself why the police force is so insecure. Institutions cannot be built or resources added without the right leadership in place. There are very talented officers across ranks who are stagnating and are vulnerable to vicious annual confidential reports that may block their growth The government needs to help create an enabling environment that encourages freer expression and communication within the police department to ensure best solutions. He must encourage out-of-the-box thinking and allow differing viewpoints for creativity and ownership to emerge.

The implementation of the Supreme Court order on police reforms, namely non-partisan selection for leadership positions, constituting security commissions to include the leader of the opposition and civil society, fixed tenures with accountability in performance, separation of law and order from investigation duties, and setting up of establishment boards could be the opening account of the government, along with strengthening the anti-terror mechanism such as creation of the Federal Agency, spreading the NSG to other cities and stronger law.

It is suggested that the government listen to police chiefs on a one-to-one basis, without the intervention of the bureaucracy, namely their bosses, the chief secretaries. It is also necessary to restore the positions that have been usurped by other administrative services to the police cadre. For starters, why not consider appointment of the best and senior most police officer as the union home secretary and encourgage the states to follow suit? In most of the places even directors of police are non-police officers. The situation demands a total paradigm shift. It cannot happen with the same artisans and rusted tools.

The sine qua non of any good governance is assuring security of life and property to the citizens. To ensure this, immediate attention is required to revamp the entire system of policing and collection of intelligence. Many areas like strength, proper recruitment, effective training, reformation of substantive and procedural laws, investigative procedure, speedy court trail, satisfactory conditions of service, and provision of better communication system, modern fire arms, quality bullet-proof jackets, night vision devices, have to be attended to on priority, if the nation is serious about improving intelligence and preventing crime and violence, let alone preventing and dealing with increasing incidents of insurgency and terrorism.

In recent times the usually much maligned policemen have come in for praise, appreciation and even adoration. This is due to the valour and dedication with which the security forces fought and neutralized the barbaric terrorists at Mumbai. There is an increasing tendency on the part of powerful sections of every ruling party to meddle with the postings and transfers of police officers, investigations and even in disciplinary matters undermining the discipline, accountability, authority and hierarchy in the department. Senior officers plead helplessness. This also becomes a handy alibi or excuse for their non-performance.

When police who are expected to perform their duties objectively and impartially are perceived as tools in the hands of those in power, people lose their faith and trust in them and hence do not extend cooperation. Unless the police enjoy respect and confidence of the public they will not be able to collect basic intelligence, prevent, detect or successfully prosecute criminals. If they cannot effectively deal with even ordinary crime and law and order situations, how are they going to deal with insurgency and terrorism?

The foremost task before the nation is to insulate the police force from undue influence from outside and make them accountable and responsible as instruments of law to regain the confidence of the public. Unless the credibility and effectiveness of the police are restored, as it happened in the UK, the fight against terrorism cannot succeed.

Rivalry between intelligence agencies

India is paying a heavy price for differences among its intelligence agencies as they rarely exchange inputs among themselves. The Mumbai terror attack is a case in point, say insiders. The country has three main intelligence agencies— the Intelligence Bureau (IB) for collection of internal and counter intelligence, the Research and Analysis Wing (RAW) for external intelligence, and Military Intelligence (MI) that collects military-related inputs. Rivalry between the three major intelligence agencies, RAW, IB and MI, has done a lot of damage not only to the agencies but also to the nation. The reluctance to share intelligence is the bane of all agencies, at least in India. Major General (retd) V.K. Singh, who has retired from RAW has written in his book "Raw and inside story", the proclivity to take the credit has given rise to the unpardonable trend in every agency of keeping vital intelligence close to its chest until it is disclosed to someone important enough in the political hierarchy, sometime even the prime minister. An Indian recruited by a foreign militant group is definitely the concern of the IB. When he is taken across the border for training he becomes the interest of RAW. When he re-enters India and carries out strikes against the military installations in Jammu and Kashmir, it becomes the worry of MI. Should he be handed over from one agency to the other every time he crosses a border, or should all keep a watch on him together? Should the army and IB be allowed to monitor trans-border radio and satellite links which strictly fall within the purview of RAW? These are the questions that have no clear answer and only add to the blame game between the intelligence agencies." According to former IB joint director Maloy Krishna Dhar, RAW's reluctance to share information with the IB is legendary. There have also been instances where personality clashes have deterred effective coordination between the national security advisor (NSA) and RAW chiefs. A.K. Mitra former director general of the Border Security Force (BSF), said: 'Not sharing intelligence information is a problem between all the agencies.' There is no justification for holding the critical information and not sharing the same with other agencies or security establishments. The nation is paying a price for it. If we want to thwart terror attacks, we must pull up our socks and bring the guilty officers to book, Mitra told IANS. After the Nov 26 terror attack on Mumbai that lasted 60 hours and in which 172 people were killed, the three agencies took potshots at each other. RAW and IB claimed they had given information specifying the places and the time when the terrorists could strike. But the state government and the navy denied any actionable inputs. The cabinet secretary is now looking into the matter. According to government sources, the Joint Committee of Intelligence (JIC), which analyses intelligence data from the IB, RAW and the directorates of military, naval and air intelligence and works under the National Security Council, has failed to live up to expectations. 'It is almost defunct and the chiefs of intelligence agencies have very rarely met under the JIC roof in the last two years', said a source.

Transnational terror

In the 2000s, India has been the victim of at least four major attacks by Pakistan-based terrorists: the Parliament attack in 2001, explosions on Mumbai trains in 2006, embassy bombing in Kabul in 2008 and the recent Mumbai carnage. What can India do to protect itself against future attacks? In broad terms, there are two options: stop the terror at source and tighten security at home. Let us carefully examine each of these options. There are three immediate avenues to tackling the terror at source, First, India could go on a limited war with Pakistan. While this option may help India avenge the attacks it has suffered, it is unlikely to persuade Pakistan to dismantle the terrorist outfits. On the contrary, it is likely to increase public sympathy for the outfits, make future recruitment of terrorists easier and give Pakistani army an easy exit from fighting the Taliban alongside the US army. The second avenue is Israeli-style targeted attacks at terrorist training comps. While this is a possible future option,

India's current intelligence gathering capability and ability to strike targets with pinpoint accuracy do not justify recourse to it. There is real possibility that such attempts may result in hits on civilian targets. This could do serious damage to the international goodwill India currently enjoys and would likely strengthen the hand of the terrorist outfits. The third avenue is diplomatic and seeks Pakistani cooperation in dismantling the terrorist outfits. This avenue is being currently tried with, at best marginal success. While India should keep pressing Pakistan directly and through the US, any expectation that these efforts will result in significant reduction in support for the outfits would be unrealistic. The army and ISI, which hold the keys to power in Pakistan, have been the sponsors of these outfits. They support them and are also aware that as long as the US needs Pakistan's cooperation in combating the Taliban and AI Qaeda, it will not unduly press it. No doubt, the vast coastline, the presence of terrorist outfits in a neighbouring country, the ease with which potential terrorists can blend into domestic population, the high density of population and the low appetite of Indians for searches and security alerts make India's task harder than that of the US. Nevertheless, tightening security from the current, extremely lax levels offers considerable scope for preventing many though not all potential attacks, and for capping the loss of life when attacks do actually happen. In the longer run, most potent weapon to combat terrorism at source is going to be rapid economic growth and prosperity. Intellectuals and thoughtful leaders in Pakistan recognize that economically their country is rapidly losing out to India. They also understand that India's economic achievements are well within Pakistan's grasp. Therefore, they would like to see Pakistan set aside the differences with India and move forward on the economic front. The rapprochement between the two countries during the last several years owed much to this recognition. If India can sustain its growth momentum, in less than a decade, the army in Pakistan too would come to appreciate the high cost of patronage to terrorist outfits and the large benefits peace can bring. It is precisely this possibility that the terrorist outfits fear most and therefore strike at the heart of India's prosperity.

Act with caution

Two major steps have been taken by the government to add extra teeth to its efforts to win the war on terror. A new federal agency has been proposed to exclusively investigate terror crimes. Amendments to provisions of the Unlawful Activities (Prevention) Act (UAPA) have been suggested to strengthen the legal system against terrorist acts. We commend the government for acting swiftly to ensure that the fight against terrorists is not handicapped by a lack of adequate systemic infrastructure or by loopholes in the legal set up. However checks should be put in place to ensure that agencies responsible for carrying out the nation's battle with terrorism do not overstep their briefs. The National Investigation Agency (NIA) Bill 2008 calls for establishing a federal agency, with exclusive powers to investigate terror crimes. At first glance, the function of the NIA and the CBI, a central agency that primarily investigates corruption cases, could overlap since the funding of terror networks are mainly through hawala transactions and other illegal means. Parliament should therefore debate whether the CBI could be merged with the NIA. This might help the government make better use of facilities available with the CBI. It takes time and resources to build a new organisation. The nation is short of time in its war against terrorism. Some of the proposed amendments to UAPA curtail rights of citizens guaranteed by the Constitution and could be argued against. It is necessary, that debates on these controversial provisions take into account the difficult times we are in. This nation is in a state of war. This war waged by ideologically motivated transnational outfits is unlike conventional wars fought between armies. The nation has to fight without even formally declaring a war. The proposed provisions in UAPA are part of a war strategy. They may scar the liberal face of this democratic country. But we do not have a choice considering the unconventional nature of the enemy and the extraordinary circumstances in which the war is being waged.

However, our lawmakers should recognise that the limits imposed on certain freedoms of the citizen could only be a temporary measure, and legislate accordingly. It is impossible to guess a time frame for the conclusion of a war on terror. But Parliament should have a periodic review, perhaps annual, of UAPA even though it is a permanent law. Anti-terror laws like TADA and POTA were rolled back after complaints of abuse. An all-party parliamentary committee should monitor the implementation of UAPA and, if necessary, annul provisions that are obviously abused. The government should also move fast on police and legal reforms to bring institutional checks against possible excesses of laws like UAPA.

Tighten the security holes

The government has finally put security reforms on a fast track. They have announced a Bill to set up a National Investigating Agency, a new coastal command, amending the CISF Act to protect private facilities and a slew of other measures. The three key areas for reform are: intelligence gathering and communication, specialist training and equipment and coordination between the federal and state ministries concerned. The first of these areas has received the greatest attention. A federal investigative authority alone may not be sufficient to reform our security. We need an authority which can, at the least, oversee the reforms that are required in our armed forces, coast guard, police and intelligence agencies as well as in our financial and cellular services. If those reforms are to be separately undertaken by the concerned ministries, then we need to hear what they will be and on what time frame. Logically, they should be simultaneous and the reforms should be integrated in order to facilitate interoperability in times of crisis. Otherwise it will be impossible to coordinate between intelligence and action, a scenario that we are all too familiar with.

CBI & FBI of United States

When we examine the working of our pioneer investigating agency CBI, is it perfect or infallible, how can it be made the best instrument in countering and investigating the increasing menace of crime that threaten the nations integrity, security and economic stability? The recommendation of the parliamentary panel to bestow on CBI the same status as the FBI of the US has focused attention. In 1977, in the Hawala Case, after noticing the report of the Independent Review Committee of the Central Government, the Apex court has strongly advocated insulation of the CBI from executive, political and extraneous influence. One of the suggestions of the standing committee is empowering the CBI to *suo-motu* investigate the case where national, security or integrity is in danger. A long felt need is to classify certain crimes affecting national security and economy, like terrorism, espionage, drug and human trafficking, cyber crime, money laundering, counterfeit currency and similar serious and complex crimes involving many states and even countries classified as federal crimes. The main advantage would be for the central investigating agency to come into picture immediately when the crime comes to light. Presently most of the terrorist related and complex investigations are being handed over to the CBI after valuable time is lost.

The CBI works as per the Delhi Special Police Establishment Act 1946, which means the central government exercises superintendence over it. Functioning of the CBI in the states is contingent upon the respective states granting consent to it. Under the existing constitutional arrangement police and public order are states subject. By virtue of that politically all the executive and legislative powers covering criminal investigation are vested with the state government agency. Entry 8 of the Union list mentions Central Bureau of Intelligence and Investigation. Hence consent of the state government is required before the CBI can be entrusted with the investigation of any offence. Due to Sec. 6 of the Delhi Special Police Establishment Act 1946, the CBI cannot on its own investigate those cases. The states are reluctant to give such consent, particularly if the centre and the state are ruled by different political parties.

The CBI lacks independence, infrastructure and legal competence to engage in tasks like FBI, which was established in 1908 as Bureau of investigation. Under 1968 legislation its directors are appointed by the US president subject to confirmation by the U.S. senate and the maximum tenure is fixed as 10 years. Under the 2001 Patriot Act, the FBI has the legal authority for wire trapping and monitoring of internet activity. Under its so-called "Sneak and pick" provision, the FBI can search premises in the absence of residents and not notify them even afterwards. The FBI was then armed with greater authority by virtue of Intelligence Authorisation Act 2004, which gave it unprecedented power to secure information from financial institutions without authority from the court.

In the United States, FBI comes into the picture whenever offences classified as federal crimes are committed. In view of the growing menace of terrorism, narco terrorism and economic crime a consensus can be created. The States have to be assured and convinced that such powers will not be misused and shall only be used in the national interest. Need of the hour is a well equipped investigating agency that can galvanize itself for action all over the country so as to deal with terrorism and high-tech crimes.

National Investigation Agency Bill

The National Investigation Agency Bill and Unlawful Activities (Prevention) Amendment Bill were introduced in both houses of Parliament on Dec. 6, 2008 within less than three weeks of the gruesome events in Mumbai, and passed by the Lok Sabha the very next day.

One is unable to recall any earlier instance of important and substantive legislation, especially one bearing on the life, security, liberties and rights of the citizen, running the entire gamut of the drafting process, cabinet approval, parliamentary procedures and debate and voting on the floor of the House, within such a remarkable short time.

By passing the said Bill the government has shed the past inhibitions and started inching forward in the ruthless, relentless and remorseless manner in which countries like US and UK, with far longer and stronger democratic tradition than India's had been successfully doing. The bill lacks the provision requiring the courts to treat as admissible evidence confessions made to a police officers, when such a provision already exists in the Narcotics Drugs and Psychotropic substance Act, Foreign Exchange Management Act and the Maharashtra Control of Organised Crime Act. The bill has gone too far by extending the period of custody without bail from 90 days to 6 months and by encroaching on the rights of the state in respect of prevention and investigation of crimes and maintenance of law and order. These provisions may be misused. On the whole the government has done a right thing in putting on the statute book the long needed legislation to set up a national investigation agency and strengthen the Act with more stringent provision. It is claimed that the Act certainly maintains a fair balance between respect of fundamental human rights and the need for tough laws.

Imitating FBI model of USA won't work for India. Every solution occurs within a particular resource configuration. Simply saying that America has prevented attacks after 9/11, and therefore we must do what America is doing is not correct. America does not have Pakistan, the epicenter of global terrorism as its immediate neighbour. The annual budget of FBI is also much more than our CBI. Efforts to imitate American solutions have already created a number of dysfunctional agencies like the National Security Council, Defence Intelligence Agency, National Disaster Management Authority and others.

One too many

Following the outcry yet again against wastage of manpower for VIP security following the Mumbai terror attacks, there are reports of a relooking at the entire system of providing security at public expense. This is nothing new; such exercises have been undertaken on numerous occasions earlier, without any real impact.

A similar exercise was undertaken three years ago in January 2006 by the home ministry. Under consideration then was also a proposal to make VIPs pay for their security, fully or partially. Nothing came of it. Providing state security to “very important persons” whose security is a matter of national or state concern is an accepted state function. The memory of what the nation faced when a member of her own security outfit killed Prime Minister Indira Gandhi in 1984 is still fresh. Twenty five years on, the nation is yet to come to terms with the aftermath and trauma of that event. More recent was the stark reality of the attack on India’s Parliament in December 2001.

As the people’s representative, a chief minister or one holding a public office, often compromises his or her personal safety in order to carry out the business of government. There is no doubt lives of some public personalities, especially the likes of members of the Gandhi family and leader of opposition L K Advani, can often be at grave risk. Many others figure on hit lists of terrorists, have received oral or written threats from fringe elements, even from cranks whose threats cannot be ignored.

The fact that a public functionary’s job involves functions and decision making in the public interest that cannot possibly please both the ‘pro’ and the ‘against’ elements is reason enough to render him potentially vulnerable. Hence the need to put in place all possible security measures to safeguard against violent attacks.

It is also true that even the ordinary citizen in India has become vulnerable and security conscious. Over time, the realisation has dawned that society’s primary security provider —

the police — is really not in a position to give protection to all people individually at all times. A fine distinction is emerging between the concepts of "security for individuals per se" and the overall umbrella of "collective security" which the police are responsible for.

Politicians constitute the biggest chunk of the so-called 'endangered lot'. Security to them has to be provided not just when in power but at times also after they have demitted office. The threat could often be on account of the politician's own misdeeds or his criminal record, which is not uncommon in India.

Security is provided on the basis of threat perception assessed by intelligence agencies, but this, the public feels, is often doctored to provide the individual higher security than he actually needs. There is also a category of persons for whom gun-totting commandos and a VIP red light on the hood of the armoured car are status symbols — they add to the person's aura.

When the list of security-seekers extends to every sundry politician and bureaucrat, his kith and kin and socialites and activists, the business of "keeping VIPs safe" becomes a drain on the national exchequer. If a majority of this lot were made to pay from their pocket, there would be a more realistic assessment of the perceived threat.

Out of Delhi Police's (DP) overall strength of 65,000 personnel, only 20,000 are deployed in police stations directly to protect and police 1.6 million people in Delhi's 11 districts. Against this, the fact is that over 7,000 policemen from DP's security unit provided security till recently to 350 VIPs.

More personnel from DP's armed battalions are often deputed to meet the ministry's additional orders to provide security cover to persons outside this list too. The 'worthies' are assessed for the type of security to be provided — from the low grade X to Y class to the Z, Z+ and Z++ category depending on the threat perception.

And personnel from the country's central paramilitary forces — over 2000 in number — are at DP's disposal to guard VIP residences in addition to the security personnel deployed. The Special Protection Group that primarily guards the prime minister, former prime ministers and their family members has over the years grown from 800 personnel in 1985 to 3,000 and yet is reportedly understaffed to meet security demands.

Central forces like the ITBP, CRPF and NSG are also hard-pressed because of VIP duty. Colossal amounts of taxpayers money goes into the security paraphernalia designed to guard these VIPs, most of whom can afford to pay for their security.

Among areas that need a re-look is also the colossal manpower wastage for the VIP's route, lining and stopping of traffic at intersections. Why should traffic be stopped for the lieutenant-governor and other VIPs at traffic light signals in Delhi?

It is time the home ministry frames a policy for providing a realistic state security; to provide it to only the highest offices in the country; to those who've come under actual threat in the discharge of their official duties alone, and not to pseudo, devious or pompous status-seekers.

Police reforms

On November 25, 2008, Julu Yadav fought terrorists with an unwieldy .303 rifle. Elsewhere, the D.B. Marg Police station staff in the Chhatrapati Shivaji Railway Station in Mumbai, overcame heavily armed terrorists with 9 min pistols and lathis. Several personnel were killed and injured in the encounters. A senior police inspector proudly said of his men: "We didn't have weapons but we had guts."

These revelations after the recent Mumbai terror attacks have created a frenzy of accusations over what is wrong with our policing.

Julu Yadav defended a huge railway station with an ancient .303 he hadn't fired for years. He couldn't get the terrorists, not because he failed. He failed to get them because he was too brave and his leadership in the force and in the government were too cowardly to face up to the needs of the nation and give up their own selfishness. No amount of draconian legislation or patriotic bombast will solve the security needs of ordinary citizens, who continue to face the brunt of terrorist attacks, bad policing and poor governance.

Rationalising arrest laws

Lost in the flurry of the Bills hastily passed by Parliament, the most significant changes relate to the law of arrest, with the new provisions going someway towards balancing the requirement of effective law enforcement with the necessity of protecting people from injustice and police harassment. Before the amendment, Section 41 of the CrPC permitted the police to arrest without warrant "any person who has been concerned with any cognisable offence," even on the mere presence of "reasonable suspicion." The new provisions stipulate that for cognisable offences punishable with a maximum imprisonment of less than seven years, arrests should be made only against the existence of "credible information" or a "reasonable complaint." The police, moreover, are obliged to record in writing the reasons for making such arrests, which are permitted only under certain conditions, for example, to prevent the person from committing further crimes or tampering with evidence. When arrest is not justified under these conditions, the police may only issue a notice of appearance: asking the presence of a person suspected of the crime to appear before it or at any other specified place.

Other safeguards against the vast discretionary powers of the police are stricter procedures during the making of an arrest, the introduction of regular medical examination of those in police custody, and the establishment of police control rooms in all districts that must display the names and addresses of those arrested. The Code of Criminal Procedure (Amendment) Bill 2008 is based substantially on a draft prepared by the Law Commission in its

177th report and reflects the spirit of several Supreme Court judgments on the power and procedure to make arrests. The third report of the National Police Commission suggested that nearly 60 per cent of arrests were unnecessary and unjustified. It estimated that the abuse of the moving to arrest without a warrant accounted for more than 43 percent of expenditure on jails. By making this law more humane and rational, the amending Bill is an important step towards improving what the Supreme Court once described as the hallmark of a nation's civilisation the methods it uses to enforce the criminal law.

INDEX